□ □ □ □ □ □ □ □ □ □ □

## IN–HOUSE TEAM

**Editor–in–chief:** Caroline Blake

**Sub–editor:** Mike Toller

**Designer:** Anja Wohlstrom

**Editorial & design assistant:** Alc___ __

**Production consultant:** Iain Leslie

**Cover design:** James Cuddy and Jake Howard

**Sales director:** Brett MacDougall

**National advertising manager:** Sue Ostler

**Web development:** Cameron J Macphail

**Accounts and HR:** Sharon Evans

**Operations director:** Martin Dallaghan

**Managing director:** Ian Merricks

**Publisher:** IMD Group

*Thanks to Katy Georgiou, Laura Jones and all previous contributors and photographers.*

ery,
na
n,
Midgley,
Weppler,
Gareth Thornton, Joe Varley, Veronica Wood, Rachel Glover, Kim Power, Joly Braime, Tom Crush, Adam Ternent.

**Photography:** Caroline Sanders, Linda Shakesby, Kate Hargrave, Roland Eva, Rebecca Johnson, Ibon san Martin, Matthew Bowden, Jorge Nassauer, Enver Uçarer, Mark Fletcher, Mirco Delcaldo, Nathalie Dulex, Tim Ireland, Adam Elliston, Dave Tett.

Itchy Media Ltd
White Horse Yard
78 Liverpool Road
London
N1 0QD

**Tel:** 020 7288 9810
**Fax:** 020 7288 9815
**E-mail:** editor@itchymedia.co.uk
**Web:** www.itchycity.co.uk

**ISBN: 1-905705-11-5, 978-1-905705-11-5**

□□□□□□□□□□□□

# Welcome to Itchy 2006

We've trawled this green and pleasant land to bring you the finest guide to outing and abouting that our sceptred isle has to offer. We're bruised and battered after the escapades we've carried out in your honour, so the least you can do is follow our trail of destruction. Liver let die, eh? This book is bursting with cool bars, cosy pubs, lazy cafés and budget beds. We'll even tell you where to get hold of a slippery nipple at 4am. Team Itchy all have PhDs in misbehaviour; if it's debauchery you're after, we've got places to pull in and places to pass out in. The culture vultures are catered for too, from Caravaggio through to comedy. We've also done a spot of re-decorating since 2005, so we hope you like the new look. Bright and dynamic; a bit like your good selves. We've even given you shiny symbols to make your life that bit easier (have a gander below). Researched and written by locals, Itchy is your new best mate. Come on, let's get under the covers...

🕒   Opening hours

🍴   Food

🍷   House wine

£   Price

### Welcome to Leeds

So, it's official; a survey has named Leeds as the UK's sexiest city. Well, that's all very flattering, but where exactly do all these fine young lovelies hang out? If only you knew that, you could prevent a reoccurrence of the alcohol-fuelled horrors of last Friday night, when you went out on the pull only to wake up the next morning in a compromising position with that Big Issue seller. My God, those warts looked ferocious in the cold light of day...

Well, never fear. Itchy is at hand to help you skip past pubbing

pitfalls, laugh in the face of bar blunders, karate chop clubbing catastrophes, and side-step those shopping disasters. Meet your new best friend. Aaaah. As well as knowing all the trendiest shops to go to during the day, your pocket-sized companion makes an ideal drinking buddy at night. We're like Jimmy 'Five Bellies' to your Paul Gascoigne. Only in a good way. We'll introduce you to the city's coolest drinking dens without getting all maudlin after one too many G&Ts and starting to blub like a big girl's blouse as we belt out 'I Will Survive' on the karaoke. And let's face it, as the city receives accolade after accolade, new venues are opening up faster than Zack Dingle downs pints in the Woolpack, so you're going to need a bit of help.

With fantastic new restaurants like the Angel's Share in Chapel Allerton and cutting-edge clubs like Wire opening in the past year, you don't want to be wasting your time in places where the rabid staff are liable to bite you if you have the audacity to ask for a drink. With your faithful Itchy guide, you need never find yourself scratching your head for something to do. Don't leave home without it. Well, unless you enjoyed the warts experience that is. In which case, you are one sick little puppy.

## Two hours in Leeds

Unless you want to spend your two precious hours among suicidal Leeds United fans watching their team being thrashed by the likes of Crewe Alexandra, here are a couple of handy hints that will steer you well clear of the wailing and gnashing of teeth at Elland Road:

1) Any southerners venturing north of Watford for the first time, convinced that the best they can hope for in the wilds of Yorkshire is to get away without being mauled to death by a ferret should head in the direction of Briggate. A quick browse round Harvey Nic's will soon show you that the North can do classiness just as well as it can small nippy mammals. Stick that in your stereotype and smoke it. Then pop over to the Corn Exchange to fawn over some fancy threads.

2) Any folk venturing into the big city from outlying villages, like Bradford and Huddersfield, should head towards the City Art Gallery where you can soak up a bit of sophistication and culture. Just watch out for the big long strips of tarmac containing all the fast metal cows with wheels. They're called roads and cars, and the latter hurt when they hit you.

# Introduction

## Two days in Leeds

**STAY** – Dump your bags at 42 The Calls for top views of the River Aire. Alternatively, Malmaison offers a state-of-the-art gym as well as a bar.

**SHOP** – Try not to make yourself dizzy as you run round in circles inside the Corn Exchange handing your credit card over to any Tom, Dick or Harry standing behind a cash till in these gorgeous little boutiques.

**ACTIVITIES** – If it's sunny, you can't beat a gentle stroll around Roundhay Park. However, if hail stones the size of golf balls are flinging themselves from the heavens killing small dogs and children, why not take refuge inside the West Yorkshire Playhouse?

**EAT** – If you fancy some posh nosh, you can trough yourself silly at Chapel Allerton's Angel's Share. If an eat-as-much-as-you-can is more your style, you can't beat a Chinese at Maxi's in the Light.

**DRINK** – For a cocktail list as long as the BFG's arm, try Prohibition on Greek Street.

**CLUB** – Wire is the place to go if you like to swim against the mainstream, whereas Mission will serve the needs of those of you who like to cram as many beats per minute as possible into their nights out.

## Two days on the cheap

**STAY** – If you don't fancy kipping in the train station while that tramp with Tourette's is doing the rounds, and the idea of setting up your tent in Roundhay Park is even less appealing, your best bet is to head towards Cardigan Road where you'll find a stack of bargainous B&Bs to kip over in.

**SHOP** – If you're brassick, steer well clear of Harvey Nic's and the Victoria Quarter. No one likes to see grown men and women cry in public. You're going to have to go for some secondhand threads instead. Try your luck in Sugar Shack in Headingly or The Final Curtain across the road.

**ACTIVITIES** – The Royal Armouries is full of all sorts of war-mongering contraptions. Get yourself some replica swords and make like Zorro. Huzzah!

**EAT** – You can't beat Wetherspoons for cheap grub. Two meals for £5.

**DRINK** – And you can't beat Wetherspoons for cheap booze either. Jugs and shooters at bargain-bucket prices.

**CLUB** – Get to Baja Beach Club before 10pm and you can ogle the bar staff wearing their swimming cossies.

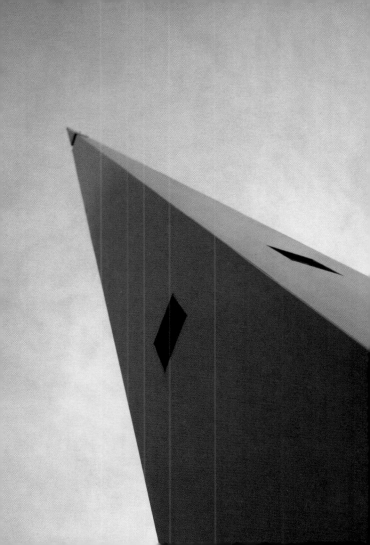

# LATIN LIFE

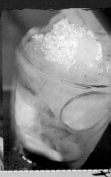

Open all day
for lunch,
dinner, tapas
& cocktails.

Come in and
enjoy a taste
of Latin Life.

Happy Hour 12.00-
7.30pm & all day
Sunday & Monday

## 20% OFF FOOD

DUNCAN ST. CORN EXCHANGE
CLOTH HALL ST.
CALL LANE
CROWN ST.
ASSEMBLY ST.
BRIGGATE
THE

# EAT IT DRINK IT FEEL IT LIVE IT

Cloth Hall Street, Leeds  0113 243 9533

menus & booking online:
www.iguanas.co.uk

LAS IGUANAS

RESTAURANT & CACHAÇARI

Eat

# Eat

## CAFÉS

### Brodicks

**Lower Level, Corn Exchange**
**(0113) 245 5190**

You don't go to Brodicks for the food. The sandwiches are ok, but the secret to this café's success is its fabulous location, slap-bang in the middle of the Corn Exchange. Absolutely fantastic for a bit of people watching. It also means you don't have to stagger far with all those shopping bags when you suddenly come over a little faint after realising you've just spent an entire month's wages in the space of half an hour, and spending more on food is the only answer.

Ⓒ *Mon–Sat, 10am–5pm; Sun, 10am–4pm*
Ⓝ *Swedish meatball ciabatta roll, £3.95*

### Caffé Nero

**19 Albion Place**
**(0113) 243 8820**

For those rare days when we do actually get some sunshine, you can enjoy the most important meal of the day sitting outside. They do a great choice of coffees and pastries for when you just can't face that fry-up. Alternatively, you're so tired that you can't go on without your caffeine fix, you can pump yourself so full of the stuff that you'll be jittering your way down the road gnashing your teeth so hard that you'll be needing permanent dental reconstructive surgery. Or you could save the hassle and go for a decent smoothie instead.

Ⓒ *Mon–Fri, 7am–7pm; Sat, 8am–7pm*
Ⓝ *Panini, £3–4*

### Citrus

**13a North Lane**
**(0113) 274 9002**

This sophisticated and student-friendly café/restaurant has so many qualities worthy of note that the constraints of language start to become a problem. Pick your favourite complimentary adjectives and apply them to: the choice/value/taste of the food; the speed/friendliness of the service; the competence/sexual allure of the staff; the cleanliness of the décor (toilets included); the well-stocked bar and the background music. You get the idea.

Ⓒ *Mon–Sun, 9am–4pm & 5.30pm–10pm;*
Ⓝ *Pan-fried escalope of pork loin with Austrian Marsala wine sauce, £9.95*
Ⓥ *£8.95*

## Citrus Café

**Corn Exchange**

**(0113) 244 4809**

Running around shopping in circles in the Corn Exchange is enough to make anyone dizzy. So why not regain your composure over coffee and cake in the trendy Citrus Café? It's simple, it's convenient, it's stylish, and it's not over-priced. It's also a veritable celebrity hot pot. Those eloquent Transylvanian poets, the Cheeky Girls, have been spotted hanging out here. You never know, if you loiter long enough, you might even catch a glimpse of Justine from Big Brother 4. Oh yeah, life don't get much more exciting than that.

🕒 *Mon–Sun, 9am–5pm*

🍴 *Chicken burger, £4.75*

## Crusty Bin

**The Parade, North Lane, Headingley**

**(0113) 275 2558**

People with hangovers have an insatiable desire for bacon. Well, except veggies. With an overwhelming student population, Headingley is never short of hung over people. Each day, they cram like extras from a Romero movie towards the Bin to devour fry-ups. Crusty Bin also deserves a round of applause for its name. Too often the reserve of hairdressers and chip shops, it's good to see a café get in on the act of adopting a pun-based title and it's even better to see homage paid to Ted Rogers' baffling game show *3-2-1*.

🕒 *Mon–Sun, 5am–3pm*

🍴 *English breakfast, £3*

## The Clock Café

**16a Headingly Lane, Hyde Park**

**(0113) 294 5464**

Slap-bang in the middle of student central, this quirky, colourful, retro-style café offers the perfect excuse to get out of the flea pit you call home. They'll tempt you with a light-but-tasty menu, including an array of classic salads, creative ciabattas and top-notch sandwiches, as well as that culinary classic, curly fries with cheese. And if you're feeling guilty about eating out, because you're spending money quicker than Elton in a pink paint shop, your extravagance will be justified by the thought that you're probably actually getting fitter by the minute for every chomp you take.

🕒 *Mon–Sat, 10am–12am, Sun, 10am–10pm*

🍴 *Mini meze platter, £4.50*

# Eat

## Dare

**49 Otley Road**

**(0113) 230 2828**

Imagine Morecambe without Wise. Cannon sans Ball. Little minus Large. Sometimes it takes two to fulfil potential and the geniuses at Dare have come up with the perfect foil for the traditional British fry-up. Their breakfast comes to you sizzling on a skillet. Why is this so much more exciting than if it was on a plate? Perhaps it's the thrill of some steamy action over brekkie? Whatever the appeal, it works. And as if this signature dish wasn't enough, Dare serves a whole menu's worth of other tasty lunches and snacks too. Dare you not to eat here.

🕑 *Mon–Thu, 8.45am–4.30pm & 5.30–10pm; Fri–Sat, 8.45am–4.30pm & 6–10pm*

🍴 *Main meal and a drink, £6.45*

## Fat Chops

**396 Kirkstall Road**

**(0113) 275 2266**

Miles out of the city centre in the wastelands of Kirkstall, this bright café is a handy stop-off after a morning in the spy shop. If you're not known for you will power, you should probably avoid this place. Otherwise, the chances are you will end up with Fat Chops. Serving a great range of tempting food and drink, the staff here will go out of their way to accommodate even the pickiest diners. Make like a Hollywood star and try your luck for an egg white omelette

🕑 *Mon, 10am–5pm; Tue–Fri, 9am–5.30pm; Sat, 9am–5pm; Sun, 11am–4pm*

🍴 *Salsa and mozzarella panini, £3.75*

🍽 *£9.00*

## Harvey Nichols Café

**107–111 Briggate**

**(0113) 204 8000**

Intrepid shopper, untold treasure awaits you in the upper echelons of this department store; namely freshly brewed coffee and fab orange flapjacks. But be warned your path is fraught with danger. The café fortress is watched over by the ferocious Orange Ladies. They circulate the entrance with their fragrant potions, blocking your every move with their sales pitches and sprays of noxious gases. Beware, one spray to the eyes will leave you blind and vulnerable. Only those who are strong of will and fat of wallet will succeed

🕑 *Mon–Wed, 10am–6pm; Thu–Fri, 10am–11pm; Sat, 9am–11pm*

🍴 *Two courses, £14*

## Indie Joze

**6 York Place**

**(0113) 245 3192**

If you know your history, you'll know that Indie Joze once ruled the Victoria Quarter. One hefty court case later, it's back in business. With Baby Jupiter neighbouring, this is the business district's trendiest bit. The café features the same larger-than-life owner as before, seeking to make it 'the granddaddy of all bars'. With quality food, a soothing atmosphere, breezy interior, fine service, tasteful music and heaps of booze, this place just can't fail. Prepare to be the messiest you've ever been in a café.

*Mon–Fri,12pm–8pm; Food, Mon–Fri, 12pm–3pm*

*Jerk chicken, £5.65*

*£9.95*

## Kadas

**Crown Street**

**(0113) 243 3433**

Late-night chill-out/pig-out zone serving a variety of North-African-inspired dishes – all with lashings of hummus. Conveniently located within crawling distance of the bars of Call Lane, this place has plenty of fancy cushions to collapse into. The perfect place to recuperate at the end of a full-tilt night on the town. The only problem you're going to have is forcing yourself back into those torturous stilettos and out into the cold to search for that elusive taxi home. We're sure they can shoe-horn you out of that sofa somehow. Anyone got a winch?

*Mon–Sat, 11am–late; Sun, 12pm–1am*

*Toasted sandwich, £3.50*

## Sahara

**East Gate**

**(0113) 253 6067**

Sleepy atmosphere, tasty Middle-Eastern cuisine and plenty of cheap cups of tea make Sahara an ideal spot for long philosophical discussions about the meaning of life and who should be kicked out of Big Brother. The café that is, not the desert. All that sand being blown into your mouth every time you tried to speak might make that difficult. Long opening hours mean you can pop in day or night. So why not give the kebab shop a miss and go for a fruity sheesha instead? You can pretend you're on a vague health kick. Breathe in mint, breathe out baccy.

*Mon–Sun, 10am–4am*

*Fruit sheesha, £5*

# Eat

## RESTAURANTS

### 56 Oriental Restaurant
**56 Wellington Street**
(0113) 245 0380

Meet the most efficient staff in Leeds. We have a sneaking suspicion that they're really huge soldier ants in disguise, running around in single file, delivering noodles to all who come. How else could they manage to keep this place running like clockwork and incredibly clean? Ok, maybe we need to lay off the sake, but this really is one of the best oriental restaurants in Leeds.

ⓒ *Mon–Sun, 12pm–2.30pm; Mon–Fri, 5pm–11pm; Sat, 6pm–11pm; Sun, 6pm–10.30pm*

ⓘ *Malaysian curry, £7.95*

ⓩ *£9.95*

### Aagrah
**St Peter's Square, Quarry Hill**
(0113) 245 5667

Spawned in Shipley in 1977, Aagrah finally hit the big city in 2004. Not your average Indian, it's got a swanky interior. Even the toilets are smart – fit for Tendulkar. Chuck in attentive service with a buzzing atmosphere and you've got yourself a great dining experience. The menu offers a stack of treats, including a whole stuffed lamb for £200, serving 15 people (*Hello Dolly* seems appropriate with The Playhouse nearby). There's plenty for those born in Vegetaria too. For the thrifty, there's the pre-theatre deal Sunday to Thursday. And the food? First-rate.

ⓒ *Mon–Sat, 5.30pm–12am Sun, 5.30pm–11pm*

ⓘ *Murgh makhani and pilau rice, £9.30*

ⓩ *£9.95*

### Akbars
**15 Eastgate**
(0113) 245 6566

It might be the younger sibling of Akbars Eastgate, but it's so popular that even the Clash felt it needed celebrating in song. 'Rock the Akbars' sang Joe Strummer. At least that's what we think he was saying. The naan breads in this place are bigger than a big thing in a big-thing-making factory, and the reasonably priced food of the highest standard makes this place a credit to our city. Let's just hope they keep up all the good work they've done so far.

ⓒ *Sun–Thu, 5pm–12pm; Fri–Sat, 5pm–12.30pm*

ⓘ *Chicken tikka masala, £7.95*

ⓩ *£9.95*

■ ■ □ □ □ □ □ □ □ □ □ □

# Eat

## Arts Café

42 Call Lane

(0113) 243 8243

A vibrant little joint, bursting with character and bustling with the kind of arty bohemian types oft to be found hanging around Call Lane in smoking jackets, puffing on Gauloises and postulating about Kierkegaard. A huge range of lunchtime meals, and a separate à la carte menu in the evening, means that there is something to please all palates. Even if you're just drinking, the bar is stocked with pretty much anything you fancy. Provided you don't fancy alcopops that is.

🕒 *Mon–Wed, 12pm–10pm; Thu–Sat, 12pm–10.30pm; Sun, 10.30am–10pm*

🍴 *Lunch plates, from £5.95*

💷 *£10.50*

## Bibis Criterion

Criterion Place

(0113) 243 0905

Where do you go in Leeds if you're after a bit of glamour? Well if Bibis is stylish enough for Eddie Izzard, it's stylish enough for us. Ok, so Jimmy Saville was spotted there too, but we won't hold that against them. The food is outstanding. You might have to hang around for a while before being seated, but with a well-stocked bar serving a fantastic range of cocktails, waiting for a table has never been so much fun.

🕒 *Mon–Sat, 12pm–2.15pm; Mon & Tue, 6pm–11pm; Wed–Fri, 6pm–11.30pm; Sat, 6.30pm–11.30pm; Sun, 12pm–3.30pm & 6.30pm–10.30pm*

🍴 *Porchette salsa alle mele, £13.50*

💷 *£14.75*

## Babycream

153–155 The Headrow

(08000) 277 171

If you like a bit of house music with dinner, this could be the place for you. A range of platters are available to share with your mates. This is not an excuse to start a food fight though. Not only will you waste some exquisite chow, you'll also make a mess of all that lovely white furniture, while inflicting untold trauma on the too-cool-for-school clientele. You've got to hand it to Babycream, it's not everywhere that can pull off a glow-in-the-dark reindeer.

🕒 *Mon–Sun, 12pm–2.45pm; Sun–Thu, 6pm–10pm*

🍴 *The worldwide, £12.95*

💷 *£13.50*

# Eat

## Brasserie Forty 4

**42–44 The Calls**

**(0113) 234 3232**

Brasserie Forty 4 are keen to let everyone know that their venue is popular with 'personalities from television, stage, music and sport'. So before you go down there, try to compose yourself. We don't want you getting all excited and spilling cheesecake down your best frock just because you happen to catch a glimpse of Cain Dingle from Emmerdale. Seriously, this food is too good to waste, and with some bargainous fixed-price menus on the go, even us mere mortals can afford to indulge ourselves.

☺ *Mon–Thu, 12pm–2pm & 6–10.30pm; Fri, 12pm–2pm & 6pm–11pm; Sat, 6pm–11pm*

🍴 *Rabbit casserole, £12.75*

💲 *£14.95*

## Brown's

**The Light, The Headrow**

**(0113) 243 9353**

Brown's new menu is positively medieval. Anyone for suckling pig? It's a great place for wining and dining on a budget. But be warned: it gets very noisy, so it's probably not the best place to break it to your boyfriend of ten years that you're running off with your t'ai chi instructor. With all that background noise, you'll just get your wires crossed and by the end of the evening you might find you've inadvertently agreed to marry him and move in with his mum and dad.

☺ *Mon–Sat, 11am–11pm; Sun, 12pm–10.30pm*

🍴 *Salmon fishcakes, £8.25*

💲 *£11.00*

## Café Thai

**Chinatown shopping arcade**

**(0800) 083 5552**

A sort of Thai embassy in the heart of Leeds's little Chinatown, Café Thai exists on the laudable principle of making Thai food that Thai people would actually eat, which as any traveller knows is a far cry from the sort of greasy spaghetti with freeze-dried green prawns and soy sauce dished up by similar establishments. You can eat in the restaurant itself, or for a 'cultured' night in you can always get your food delivered to you so you can stick on the Ong Bak DVD and dream of your travels.

☺ *Tue–Sun, 12pm–10.30pm*

🍴 *Lunchtime menu, £4.95*

💲 *£7.95*

# Eat

## The Calls Grill

**36–38 The Calls**
**(0113) 245 3870**

A beautiful restaurant which screams, 'High Class', or rather, writes it lovingly using calligraphy on scented notepaper, before getting the butler to slip it discreetly into your pocket. It boasts a menu so unbelievably dreamy it could be published as a work of fiction, although you might need to take out a second mortgage to foot the bill. Still, with debt consolidation companies on 24-hour standby these days, there's never been a better time to go ahead and spoil yourself.

🕑 *Mon–Sat, 6pm–10.30pm;*
*Tue–Fri, 12pm–2pm*
🍴 *Fillet steak, £16.75*
💲 *£12*

## Chaophraya

**20a Blayds Court**
**(0113) 244 9339**

We were a bit disappointed to discover that Chaophraya is just a river in Thailand. We were hoping it might translate into some words of Eastern wisdom that would provide the key to a long and happy life. Ommmm. Ah well, you can't have it all and this place does provide excellent food, a fantastic singer and a weeping tiger. (No, not a real one. That would be a ruddy miracle.) Ease back to the trickling soundtrack, warble along to the random muzak and chow down on some top nosh.

🕑 *Mon–Sun, 12pm–3pm & 5pm–11pm*
🍴 *Thai green chicken curry, £8*
💲 *£8.95*

## Chino Latino

**Park Plaza, City Square**
**(0113) 380 4000**

This place goes from strength to strength. They've got great food, an impressive selection of drinks and a lively atmosphere. It's a fantastic place to bring your fella if he doesn't quite measure up in the looks department; with subdued lighting and dark décor, if you don't look at him directly and squint a bit you might almost be able to convince yourself you're out with Brad Pitt. Ok, you're going to have to ignore the glass eye and the dodgy comb-over...

🕑 *Mon–Fri, 7am–11am & 12.30pm–2.30pm*
*& 6.30pm–10.15pm; Sat, 7am–11am &*
*6.30pm–10.15pm; Sun, 8am–12pm*
🍴 *Scallops with lemon sauce, £13*
💲 *£9*

## Darbar

**16–17 Kirkgate**
**(0113) 246 0381**

Two Darbar factoids to impress your friends with: 1) The wooden door is 400 years old and was imported from Pakistan and 2) the restaurant is a former nightclub. So, east meets west and old meets new in Raj-stylee elegance. The food is seriously lush and comes in royal portions. Expect the usual suspects, but also make a beeline for specialist balti dishes prepared in a karahi (like a wok), which equals succulent meat to the max. A top bonus is the goodie basket, overflowing with everything from fresh strawberries to boxes of chocolates.

🕓 *Mon–Sat, 11.30am–2pm & 6pm–12am*
🍴 *Fish masala, £9.50*
💲 *£11.95*

## Ferret Hall Bistro

**2 The Parade, Headingley**
**(0113) 275 8613**

Cosy, relaxed and so charming it almost hurts, visiting Ferret Hall is like visiting old friends. Ron and Jane, the proprietors, take great pride in running this restaurant with a hands-on approach, and quite rightly so. It's a much-loved establishment, and although it's small, it's always bustling with customers, serves seriously gorgeous food and provides a decent range of vegetarian options to boot. Spit in the eye of faceless, corporate chain enterprises and discover the human element of fine dining again.

🕓 *Mon–Sun, 6pm–10pm*
🍴 *Fillet of salmon, £11.95*
💲 *£10.95*

## Firefly

**21 Park Row**
**(0113) 243 1122**

Remember when restaurants were for eating, pubs were for boozing, and clubs were for strutting? Well, Firefly is part of that breed that encourages us to do all three in one place. The noshing takes place upstairs in the relative calm of the brasserie, although there's an inevitable overspill from the metro-sexual bonanza below. Aside from their amazing lunch for a fiver deal (plus soft drink), they beat the competition purely on the basis of the fact that you can slump into a comfy sofa, snaffle a cocktail or three and watch the merchant-bankers go by.

🕓 *Mon–Sat, 12pm–11pm; Sun, 12pm–10.30pm*
🍴 *Pan-fried chicken breast with lentils, £11.95*
💲 *£10.15*

# Eat

## The Flying Pizza

**60 Street Lane**
**(0870) 266 6501**

This restaurant used to be the place to see and be seen. The north Leeds glitterati would pull up in their Ferraris and bag a table in the window, where they could smoke cigarillos and flick their hair (and that was just the men). Although the halcyon days are gone, there's still a buzz in the air. The food is consistently good and the service is impeccable, though they have yet to embrace equal opportunities and hire a female waitress. Jimmy Saville is oft seen brandishing his cigars here. Jingle jangle. You have been warned.

- **Mon–Sun, 12pm–2.30pm & 6pm–11pm**
- **Spaghetti alla vongole, £7.25**
- **£11.50**

## The Gallery at Flannels

**68–78 Vicar Lane**
**(0113) 242 8732**

Oh, come on Flannels, this just isn't fair. First, you talk us into parting with the whole of our monthly wage in exchange for your fancy designer clobber, when you know perfectly well that we only got paid three days ago, and now you go and add a restaurant to tempt our weak-willed tastebuds. Oh my God! Look at those hot chocolate soufflés! If they haven't already lured you in, go home right now and hide under your bed, before you're trying to dig out a pair of fishnets to wear to see the bank manager in the morning.

- **Fri–Sat, 10am–10pm; Sun, 11am–4pm**
- **Sirloin steak and chips, £13**
- **£11**

## Grounded

**20 New Briggate**
**(0113) 242 9442**

A quaint, quiet little place just off the high street, offering reasonably priced lunchtime and evening menus alongside an impressively large selection of international lagers. (Itchy has a weak spot for EuroBeer.) But what really makes this place special, the jewel in its crown, is the fact it has surely discovered the future of British cuisine: designer bangers and mash. You select the sausages, the potatoes and the garnish you want in a pick'n'mix fashion from an extensive list. That's the kind of Spud-U-Like we're after.

- **Mon–Sat, 11am–11pm; Sun, 12pm–5pm**
- **Bangers and mash, £8**
- **£12.50**

## Hansa's

**72–74 North Street**
**(0113) 244 4408**

This restaurant would send Channel 4's Dr Gillian McKeith into Scottish raptures. Pulses? Check. Legumes? Check. Interesting interaction of flavours, textures, colours and natural goodness? Check, check, check! Forget your brown rice and Jesus sandal stereotypes; this is sumptuous, vegetarian Gujurati cuisine. Heck, they even stock Indian organic wine. Examination of stools post-dinner? Well, that's optional (but Gillian definitely would).

🕙 *Mon–Fri, 5pm–10.30pm; Sat, 5pm–11pm; Sun, buffet lunch, 12pm–2.30pm*
🍴 *Methi bateta (potato curry with fenugreek herbs), £5.25*
🍷 *£10.50*

## Japanic

**9 Queen Square**
**(0113) 244 9550**

Not since the miraculous transformation of Plain-Jane-Super-Brain, have we seen something so delicious emerge from such an unpromising chrysalis. What was Leeds's most uninspiring pub, The Coburg, is now Japanic, a Japanese-restaurant-cum-karaoke-bar. This is a great place for the diner on a budget. Order one of the set meals, with 37 different courses to try. Perfect for greedy people with short attention spans.

🕙 *Mon–Fri, 12pm–2pm & 6pm–10pm; Sat, 12pm–3pm & 6pm–10pm; Bar, Mon–Thu, 12pm–1am; Fri–Sat, 12pm–2am*
🍴 *Beef yaki udon, £3*
🍷 *£3 for a glass*

## Hard Rock Café

**The Cube, Albion Street**
**(0113) 200 1310**

You know what to expect when you go to Hard Rock Café – fries, lots of beer, and half a cow's carcass in a bun. If you're impressed by the fact that it looks like rock'n'roll has thrown up all over the walls, we suggest you eat at night, when the Bon Jovi gets cranked up. *'Wooooooaaah! We're halfway there...'* You'll have to fight your way through lots of hairy young men in impossibly tight jeans to get to the bar. Try not to upset them by tripping over their air guitars, eh?

🕙 *Sun–Wed, 12pm–12am; Thu, 12pm–1am; Fri–Sat, 12pm–2am*
🍴 *Twisted mac, £9*
🍷 *£12.50*

# Eat

## Jino's Thai Café

**46a Otley Road**
**(0113) 278 8088**

It's a constant source of frustration to us that we've yet to come across a Thai restaurant called 'Thai a Yellow Ribbon Round the Old Oak Tree', and seeing as this one's just a stone's throw from the Original Oak pub in Headingly, we thought all our Christmases would come at once. No such luck. However, it's the prawn crackers that really make this place special. They're a million miles away from the usual bits of piss-soaked polystyrene you always get given in lesser establishments.

 Tue–Fri, 11am–2.30pm & 5pm–10pm; Sat–Sun, 12pm–4pm & 5pm–10pm

🍽 Pad Thai chicken, £5.40

🍷 BYO

## Leodis

**Victoria Mills, Sovereign Street**
**(0113) 242 1010**

If you've finally managed to convince the girl you've been after for ages to go on a date with you, don't blow it. Take her to Leodis. Despite being pretty damn classy, this restaurant is unpretentious and the staff won't look at you like a vomit-splattered tramp, even if your companion for the evening is wearing less than Abi Titmus when the paparazzi are around. However, they won't be too impressed if you can't afford to pay, and with these prices you'll be washing up until your hands bleed.

🕐 Mon–Fri, 12pm–2pm & 6pm–10pm; Sat, 6pm–11pm

🍽 Grilled swordfish steak, £14

🍷 £13.95

## Las Iguanas

**Unit 3 Cloth Hall Street**
**(0113) 243 9533**

One for the Latin lovers out there, this. The hungry among you can sample the regional South American food, including Xinxim (Pelé's favourite dish), and for those of you who like the odd Mojito, head straight for the Cachaçaria (named after Brazil's national drink). Grab yourself one of the cocktails, plonk yourself down amongst the mosaic tabletops and Latin artefacts and, but for the fact that it's probably raining, you could just as easily be in Sao Paulo as Leeds.

🕐 Mon–Thu, 12pm–11pm; Fri–Sat, 12pm–11.30pm; Sun, 12pm–10.30pm

🍽 Xinxim Brazilian lime chicken, £9

🍷 £11.50

## Livebait

**11–15 Wharf Street, The Calls**
**(0113) 244 4144**

All you old seadogs (and anyone else who happens to enjoy fresh fish, crab, lobster and the like) should get yourselves down to Livebait. With exposed brick walls and wooden floors, this is seafood done the posh way. It might be an idea to have a shave and polish your wooden leg before you set off, as you wouldn't want to be responsible for lowering the tone now would you? Oh and leave the parrot at home. Ooohh arghhhh, me hearties.

🕒 *Mon–Thu, 12pm–3pm; Mon–Thu,*
*5.45pm–10.30pm; Fri–Sat, 12pm–11pm;*
*Bar, Mon–Sat, 12pm–11pm*
🍴 *Roasted monkfish tail with port sauce, £16.95*
💷 *£11.50*

## Nando's

**Unit 4, The Light, The Headrow**
**(0113) 242 8908**

If Nando's are to be believed, the Potugese live on a diet of chicken, though we doubt Eusebio would be the size he is if he were only eating white meat. Nando's is essentially a posh KFC, substituting finger-licking for cutlery and boasting staff with less acne and better English language skills. There's a cornucopia of spicy chicken products to be had at reasonable prices. Not a bad place to drop in for a quick bite before Vue. But only if you like chicken.

🕒 *Mon–Thu, 11am–11pm; Fri–Sat,*
*11am–12am; Sun, 11am–10.30pm*
🍴 *Mediterranean chicken salad, £6*
💷 *£9.95*

## Medina

**2–4 Britannia Street**
**(0113) 242 6655**

This stylish Italian restaurant hosts all the usual culinary suspects. Well, pizza and pasta anyway, and it does so at a reasonable price. The waiters will keep your wife/girlfriend happy by showering her with all kinds of inappropriate attention, leaving you free to leer at Kylie and her impossibly pert posterior, as she parades around in yet another stunning pair of hot pants on the huge plasma screen. 'What's that dear? You're leaving me for Pablo? That's nice.'

🕒 *Mon–Fri, 12pm–2.30pm& 6pm–10.30pm;*
*Sat, 6pm–11pm; Sun, 6pm–10.30pm*
🍴 *Prosciutto pizza, £6.45*
💷 *£12.95*

# Eat

## No 3 York Place

3 York Place

(0113) 245 9922

Ooooh la la, we like this place. Surprisingly located at number three York Place, this is an elegant modern restaurant, with a spacious interior and understated decor. Fortunately, the distinct lack of imagination demonstrated in choosing the name is not mirrored in the food they serve. The menu, which has a subtle French flavour, changes once a month so you'll never get bored. Not that you'll be able to afford to eat here that often anyway.

ⓒ *Mon–Fri, 12pm–2pm & 6.30pm–10pm; Sat, 6.30pm–10pm*

ⓘ *Terrine of rabbit with leeks and foie gras, £9.95*

ⓞ *£14*

## The Old Police Station

106 Harrogate Road

(0113) 266 8999

When is a cop shop not a cop shop? Well when the developers are brought in to turn it into a flashy bar and restaurant. This could all have gone horribly wrong – who wants their rib-eye steak where they used to lock up the local ne'er do wells? Oh you do? Well there are some cells remaining to enhance your dining experience – complete with genuine wall scrawlings. The food has received fab reviews and they have a well-stocked bar. There is also a basement bar where you can frogmarch (sorry, stomp) the night away.

ⓒ *Mon–Thu, 12pm–11pm; Fri–Sat, 12pm–12am; Sun, 12pm–10pm*

ⓘ *Fillet of red mullet, £12.50*

ⓞ *£12*

## The Olive Tree

188–190 Harrogate Road

(0113) 269 8488

Yeah, ok, they may have two different entries in the Guinness bible for the longest kebab and largest milkshake respectively (milkshake? Greek?), but this is no excuse for sloppiness. This warmly-hued modern-day taverna is riding high on the Rodley branch's success; yet striving for excellence is a continual quest, not one that stops when you get an Egon Ronay award. The meze and moussaka are passable, but warm pitta bread isn't much good when it arrives so late you've finished the dips. Could do better.

ⓒ *Mon–Sun, 12pm–2pm & 6pm–10.30pm*

ⓘ *Lamb kleftiko, £11.95*

ⓞ *£12.95*

## Pietro's

10 Otley Road, Headingly

(0113) 274 4262

Pietro's is like a little place from back in the old country minus the murderous looking patrons in the corner. Too many Italian restaurants give the impression that the chef has merely opened a couple of jars of Dolmio, but this is the real deal. They probably even cut the garlic with a razor blade so that it vaporises in the pan (come on, we've all seen *Goodfellas*). It's small and cosy, rather than small and cramped and, boasts a knowledgeable staff. Not cheap, but it won't break the bank either. Belissimo.

🕒 *Tue–Thu, 6pm–10.30pm; Fri–Sat, 6pm–11pm; Sun, 6pm–10pm*

🍴 *Ravioli salmon, £7.50*

🍷 *£10.50*

## Red Chilli

1 George Street

(0113) 242 9688

The food in this place has as much in common with your usual gloopy, cardboard-y Chinese fare as the food in Harvey Nic's does with a Happy Meal. The usual suspects are on the menu (with a huge range of veggie options), but for those of you who like to experiment with food – you're not going to have the chance to practice cold fusion in here), the opportunity to try something different is so vast that you might need one of the chirpy staff to help you out. They'll hold yer hand and lead you through the epic selection.

🕒 *Sun–Thu, 12pm–11pm; Fri–Sat, 12pm–12am*

🍴 *Main courses, £7.50–15*

🍷 *£11.50*

## Salvo's

115 Otley Road

(0113) 275 5017

They have them queuing round the block to eat at this slick little eatery on the fringe of the Headingley strip. Well, not quite – they actually manage to cram everyone in – but despite the lack of elbow room, Salvo's is popular for very good reasons. A fine selection of dishes, the staple pizzas and pastas are all present and correct on the menu, as well as daily specials for the more adventurous eaters and everything is priced modestly. Best to get there early to avoid waiting for a table.

🕒 *Mon–Thu, 12pm–2pm & 6pm–10.45pm; Fri–Sat, 12pm–2pm & 5.30pm–11pm*

🍴 *Lasagne, £7.70*

🍷 *£11.95*

# Eat

## Shabab

**2 Eastgate**

**(0113) 246 8988**

A little piece of India in Leeds. Exotic décor, the aroma of freshly ground spices and the very best of eastern hospitality combine to create an experience so authentic you wouldn't bat an eyelid if an elephant walked past the window. Unfortunately, when you come to leave, with this being Leeds and not actually India, you'll probably find it's still pissing it down and the only wildlife you'll run into are the city's scallies. Still, at least whilst you're in this heavenly place you can pretend.

◉ *Mon–Fri, 11.30am–2.15pm; Sun–Thu, 5pm–11.45pm; Fri–Sat, 5pm–12.30am*

⑪ *Murgh sabz masala, £6.90*

❷ *£12.90*

## Shogun Teppanyaki

**Granary Wharf**

**(0113) 245 1856**

If you've got to the point in your relationship where you can't look at your boyfriend, let alone talk to him, Shogun Teppanyaki is for you. The chef prepares the food in full view of the customers and he's a bit of a show-off. Brandishing a machete he carves up giant squid in mid-air while performing back flips and generally doing everything your mother told you not to by a hot stove. Ok, so we might be exaggerating, but he's definitely entertaining enough to distract you from noticing just how annoying the gimp you're with is.

◉ *Mon–Sun, 12pm–2pm & 6pm–10.30pm*

⑪ *Set menu, £25*

❷ *£9.50*

## Simply Heathcotes

**Canal Wharf, Water Lane**

**(0113) 244 6611**

Generally, we Yorkshire folk are a bit wary of anything that descends on us from the wrong side of the Pennines. People who make the words 'book' and 'cook' rhyme with 'duke' and 'spook' aren't to be trusted. However, we've learnt to make an exception in the case of Lancastrian, Paul Heathcote. Located in a former grain house by the canal, his restaurant serves a mouth-watering selection of British and European dishes. A truly fabulous dining experience. Are you sure you're not one of us Paul?

◉ *Mon–Sat, 12pm–2.30pm; Mon–Fri, 6pm–10pm; Sat, 6pm–11pm; Sun, 12pm–9pm*

⑪ *Roast breast of corn-fed chicken, £16.50*

❷ *£13.95*

## Tampopo

**15 South Parade**

**(0113) 245 1816**

Let's face it, finding good pan-Asian food in a northern city is like searching for a baby prawn in a wheelbarrow of noodles – fat udon noodles at that. But we can safely brand this canteen with the itchy stamp of fusion approval. Dishes from Vietnam, Singapore, Thailand, Indonesia and Japan adorn the menu. The ubiquitous pad Thai remains a firm favourite but we recommend a pungent panang curry or an aromatic mee goreng. The service is quick, the staff are friendly and the ingredients are super-fresh.

ⓔ *Mon–Sat, 12pm–11pm; Sun, 12pm–10pm*

ⓜ *Prawn khao pad, £8.95*

ⓐ *£9.95*

## Thai Cottage

**39 Great George Street**

**(0113) 245 9224**

Good old Thai Cottage. This place is beloved of many a Leeds local. An odd, but adorable hybrid half Thai restaurant/half greasy spoon cafe, the Thai Cottage is probably the only place in Leeds to offer bacon and egg baps alongside chicken pad kee mow. And although on paper that might sound disastrous, it actually works surprisingly well (probably not on the same plate though). The staff are superb and the vibe is seriously laid-back, so open your mind and go cottaging in the Far East.

ⓔ *Mon–Sat, 7am–8pm*

ⓜ *Thai dishes, £4.50*

ⓐ *Unlicensed*

## Tariq's

**12–16 St Michael's Road**

**(0113) 275 1881**

Don't be put off by the fact that Tariq's has a siamese-twin style kebab shop attached, or that a huge percentage of their clientele seem to be pissed women crying into their kormas, because you'll be denying yourself a real treat. Perfectly sized portions, decent prices and very tasty curries in all the classic variations. There's no alcohol licence, but when half the customers are only a sip away from Bridget-Jones-style table-top karaoke, that's not necessarily a bad thing.

ⓔ *Mon–Thu, 5pm–1am; Fri–Sat, 5pm–3am; Sun, 5pm–12am*

ⓜ *Lamb balti, £5*

ⓐ *Unlicensed*

## "The Best Buffet in Town"

Oliver of Yorkshire Post

### special dedicated floor for the Buffet diners

Buffet served between 11.45 and 2.15 Mon - Fri
and from 5.30pm to 9pm Mon - Sat

Party menus, and childrens discounts available..

origina
established

**Complete**

**Fully Licensed and Air Conditioning**

**2 Eas**

## "the most authentic alacarte choice in town"

...e in an exotic setting at the oldest
...n Restaurant in the Leeds City centre.

...sit to Leeds by dining at the Shabab.

...eeds, LS2 7JL - 0113 246 8988

# Eat

## Thai Edge

**7 Calverley Street**
**(0113) 243 6333**

If you fancy bagging yourself a footballer or an actor from Emmerdale, this could be the place for you. It's not cheap but, as a wise man once said, you get what you pay for. And after you've been blown out by one of Leeds's very own minor celebrities and decided to settle for the lad you brought with you in the first place, you won't embarrass yourself by ordering something like donkey because the menu includes full English translations. Phew.

🕒 *Mon–Sat, 12pm–2.30pm; Mon–Thu,*
*5.30pm–11.30pm; Fri–Sat, 5.30pm–12am;*
*Sun, 12pm–3pm & 6pm–11pm*
🍴 *Set menu, £19.80*
💷 *£10*

## The Wardrobe

**6 St Peters Building, St Peters Square**
**(0113) 383 8800**

Interestingly placed under the Playhous costume store – where else can yo satisfy that craving for funk while dresse as Hamlet? Nestling in a corner of th mellow, spacious ground floor bar, th restaurant offers unpretentious-yet original dishes (you won't find thes chicken kievs at Asda), including a grea value pre-theatre menu. Midweek jaz ensembles often provide a toe-tappin accompaniment, although the hardcor action takes place in the downstairs club

🕒 *Mon–Fri, 9am–3pm; Sat, 12pm–3pm;*
*Mon–Sun, 5pm–10pm*
🍴 *Poached smoked haddock, £10*
💷 *£12*

## Zizzi's

**Cloth Hall Street**
**(0113) 243 5719**

Zizzi's gets mucho busy at the weekend so book in advance if you want to avoi looks of utter contempt from staff whe you wander in and ask if they happen t have a table for two. The food, when eventually arrives, is generally exceller in a chain-y sort of way and almos makes up for the crap service. If yo appreciate generous portions of goo Italian food, have time to spare and a prepared to be ignored, give this plac a bash. With a large stick if necessar

🕒 *Mon–Sat, 12pm–11pm;*
*Sun, 12pm–10.30pm*
🍴 *Calzone pizza, £7.65*
💷 *£11.95*

# FOOD FOR THOUGHT

ITCHY'S GUIDE TO FOODS THAT EVERYONE SHOULD TRY AT LEAST ONCE. GO ON, BE ADVENTUROUS. WE DARES YOU...

### Chocolate insects

Lovingly enveloped in a layer of chocolatey goodness, upmarket food stores have recently started selling these critters. You can choose from scorpion lollies or locust chews. Think, 'I'm a celebrity, get me into these...'

### Offal

While meat hysteria in the wake of the BSE crisis might discourage you from trying offal, don't be put off. Offal comes in all shapes and sizes, and although not all of you will be up to the test of courage presented by sweetbreads (glands), things such as pan-fried chicken livers are more than palatable.

### Kangaroo fillet

Whilst this steak-like meat can be a bit chewy, it's very lean and low-cholesterol. What's more, for the environmentally conscious amongst you, it may ease your conscience to know that they're not endangered and that farming them causes less damage to the environment than the farming of traditional animals. Available from your local Walkabout.

### Haggis

Take some heart, liver and lungs; mince with onion, oatmeal, suet, spices and salt. Boil in a sheep's stomach lining for several hours, and you have Scotland's most traditional dish. To not eat it would be cultural snobbery.

### Jellied eels

These little tubs of gunk are packed with so much Cockney authenticity that eating just a couple will give you the same level of East End cred as a Pearly King/Queen. Tastes like poached salmon. In slime.

# Drink

# Drink

## BARS

### The Angel's Share

**Stainbeck Corner, Harrogate Road, Chapel Allerton**
**(0113) 307 0111**

The A-team of the bar industry has come together to serve food fit for Queen Picky of Pickyville. With a menu that changes with the seasons and cocktails to knock you offa yer feet, these guys are out to impress. So, fussy drinkers, if no one else can help, and if you can find them, maybe you can hire the A-team. However, if you'd rather your Mojito wasn't knocked up in the back of a Dodge van by BA Baracus, then you could always pop along to the Angel instead.

**☺ Mon–Fri, 11am–12.30am; Sat, 10am–12.30am; Sun, 10am–11.30pm**

### The Arc

**19 Ash Road**
**(0113) 275 2223**

It's a shame that the tramp population of Headingley has chosen the benches outside The Arc as their stomping ground because sitting on the balcony under the outdoor heaters with a beer or two is a fab way to spend an evening. Still, if you can manage to ignore the loons on display, it's worth heading down there for the £3 pizza deal. And they always seem to get first dibs on the city's most attractive bar staff, which, let's face it, is never a bad thing.

**☺ Mon–Sat, 11am–12.30am; Sun, 12pm–12.30am; Food until 8pm; Selected food until 12am**
**⑪ Tagliatelle carbonara, £6.95**
**❷ £9.50**

### Arcadia Ale and Wine Bar

**Arndale Centre, Otley Road**
**(0113) 274 5599**

This is Leeds's first no-smoking bar. You have to weigh up whether being able to breathe without a gas mask makes up for the fact you'll probably find yourself surrounded by real ale drinkers all night. There's nothing more likely to put you off your pint than a pot-bellied, middle aged man with misguided facial hair. Although, if you've had all you can take from Headingley's student population, this place might be something of a haven.

**☺ Mon–Sun, 11am–11pm; Sun, 12pm–10.30pm; Food, Mon–Fri, 12pm–2pm & 6pm–8pm; Sat, 12pm–7pm; Sun, 12pm–2.30pm**
**⑪ Spicy venison sausage with mash, £6.95**
**❷ £10.45**

# ЯΣVOLUTIOП ®
## THE ELECTRIC PRESS

Situated in the recently refurbished **Electric Press Building** in the **heart of Leeds Civic Quarter**, this stunning venue offers Leeds' beautiful nightlife crowd a new destination.

By day the beautiful surroundings of our stunning patio area over looking **Leeds' Millennium Square**, while our indoor courtyard with under floor heating offers a continental urban feel for those wanting to dine inside out. Our new Revolution Kitchen Menu offers a diverse choice of dishes and is perfect for those wanting to escape from the office, dine with friends or meet for lunch with colleagues.

By night our three bars have something to offer everyone. be it sipping one of our infamous cocktail in the comfy leather booths surrounding the main bar area, dancing the night away in our eccentric caged dance floor area, or simply chilling out downstairs in our laid back retro bar area, Revolution Electric Press cannot fail to impress!

## Get your
## Privilegecard for only £3!
**save all year round!**
**great offers not to be missed**

privilegecard
ЯΣVOLUTIOП

Revolution Electric Press // 41 Cookridge Street, Leeds, LS2 3AW

# Drink

## Babycream

153 The Headrow
(0113) 380 432053

The perfect venue for a blind date. If your mystery man turns out to have the body of David Beckham and the personality of Peter Kay, Babycream's stylish décor and impressive cocktail list will distract his attention from the globule of drool dribbling down your chin. If, on the other hand, he has the body of Peter Kay and the personality of David Beckham, you won't be forced to skulk in the toilets until he finally takes the hint and leaves. Babycream has a girls-only gossip room where you can hide in style.

*Mon–Fri, 9am–2am; Sat, 10am–2am;*
*Sun, 12pm–10.30pm; Food all day*
*Chorizo chicken tortilla, £5.95*
*£13.50*

## Baby Jupiter

The Basement, 11 York Place
(0113) 242 1202

Now, here is a cult bar all right. Like stepping into an underground speakeasy, what used to be Soul Kitchen caters for the cooler cats in town. Baby Jupiter is a Leeds favourite with people in the know. Strong foreign beers, friendly bar staff and a happy bunch of locals all contribute to this tiny bar's laid-back vibe. Add to that a deliciously funky soundtrack, décor straight out of a dodgy porn film and an easy-going owner called Smurf, and you just know you're onto a winner.

*Daily, 12pm–1am; Food,*
*Mon–Fri, 12pm–2.30pm*
*Baby Jupiter platter, £4.95*
*£10.50*

## Bar Home

Arch X, Granary Wharf
(0113) 245 6555

They obviously don't believe in the mantra 'location, location, location' at Bar Home. This bar looks out onto a bleak industrial landscape that seems to have remained untouched since the mid-19th century. Bar Home makes an effort to breathe some life into the concrete graveyard that is the Wharf, and once you're inside this is a stylish bar. You just have to weigh up whether it's impressive enough to risk the walk through a tunnel that is the new venue for The Vagrants' Ideal Home Show.

*Mon–Wed, 12pm–9.30pm; Thu–Sat,*
*12pm–11pm; Food, Mon–Sat, 12pm–6pm*
*Chicken caesar salad, £3.90*
*£8*

## he Box

Jtley Road

13) 224 9266

he Box is to mullets what Spain is
migrating birds; the trendy kids of
eadingley, having adopted it as a second
ome, flock there in their thousands. If
ju've ever fancied spending an afternoon
the student union bar in Hollyoaks, this is
jobably the closest you're going to get. A
ecent night out is practically guaranteed
oviding you can cope with kitsch 80s'
ngs like *Take On Me* and *Ghostbusters*.

*Daily, 10.30am–1.30am*

*Boxster burger, £6.45*

*£8.50*

## Chino Latino

Park Plaza, City Square

(0113) 380 4000

Ever wondered what it would have
been like to be a high-flying, yuppie
stockbroker in the 80s? Well, stick some
shoulder pads in your best suit, grab
your Filofax, paint a house brick black
(that's right mobile phones really were
that big back then) and trip on down to
Chino Latino. Leave Rick Astley where he
belongs though, eh? Firmly back in 1987.

*Mon–Fri, 5pm–1am (Fri 2am); Sat,
6pm–2am; Food, 6pm–10.30pm*

*Prawn wonton, £7*

*£13*

Due to last year's re-jigging of licensing hours, you can get a drink up to the
closing times listed, but you might get some bonus drinking time too. Result! **Itchy**

# Drink

## Dr Wu's

**35 Call Lane**

**(0113) 242 7629**

Patient: Doctor, doctor, I am drawn to Call Lane but I'm sick to death of all the pretentious bars there. I have an overwhelming desire to find an intimate little joint where I can enjoy live music; the kind of place Axel Rose might visit were he in town. Doctor: Get the hell out of my consultation room and stop wasting my time. I didn't spend five years at medical school to listen to people like you moaning on when it's quite obvious you just need a good night out with my fictitious colleague Dr Wu. Honestly, next you'll be telling me you feel like a pair of curtains.

🕒 *Mon–Sat, 3pm–2am; Sun, 6pm–2am*

💰 *£9.50*

## The Elbow Room

**64 Call Lane**

**(0113) 245 7011**

It's quite a slog up the stairs to this heavenly haunt, but it's well worth the strain on your lungs. Maybe it's the rarefied atmosphere, but a low idiot quota prevails. And it's all here in paradise. You can watch the match, relax at the bar or demonstrate your trick shots on one of the 30-odd pool tables. They play indie by day and feature dance DJs at night. Angels serve the drinks (although there's no Harp) and manna comes in the form of cheesy chips. Divine.

🕒 *Mon–Sat, 12pm–2am; Sun, 12pm–12am*

🍴 *Food, Mon–Sat, 12pm–2am; Sun, 12pm–12am*

🍽 *Chips and cheese, £2.99*

💰 *£8*

# Drink

## The Faversham

**1–5 Springfield Mount**

**(0113) 243 1481**

Let's face it, when someone decided to build a bar on the fringe of the university campus, they were onto a winner. They could have stuck up a Portakabin and sold homemade dandelion wine in plastic mugs and they'd have still made a fortune. The students of Leeds have something a whole lot classier on their hands with the Fav though. Leather seating, mosaic tables and a long bar complete the funky retro feel of the place. Fantastic food, some cracking cocktails and a range of club nights mean a lot of students will probably never get round to finding out where that lecture hall is.

*Mon–Thu, 12pm–2am; Fri–Sat, 12pm–3am; Sun, 12pm–1am; Food, 12pm–6pm*

# Drink

## Firefly

**21–22 Park Row**

**(0113) 243 1122**

Apparently, Leeds is home to more accountants and solicitors than anywhere in the UK outside London. Blimey. Well this is why they need super-duper bars like Firefly to escape to after a hard day earning all that brass. Suits by day, and trendy ass shakin' Leeds goers by night. With its fab modern décor and a food menu that'd make even Gordon Ramsay smile, this is another fine place to grace the Financial District. Get there sharpish, but warn the credit card first.

Ⓒ *Brasserie & bar, Mon–Sat, 12pm–11pm; Sun, 12pm–10.30pm; Cocktail lounge, Thu–Sat, 9pm–2am; Bar menu, 12pm–1am*

Ⓜ *Pan-fried chicken breast, £13.95*

Ⓩ *£12.50*

## Fudge

25–27 Assembly Street
(0113) 234 3588

As sweet as the chocolate bar of the same name and pretty much the same size (well ok, maybe it's actually a little bit bigger than that but you get the point we're trying to make). This place is definitely worth checking out, if you can get in that is. And on a Saturday night you'll be hard pushed, because all the trendy folk of Leeds flock here as if their streaked blonde mullets depended upon it. Definitely not one for the Ben Sherman crew, as quite frankly, the bouncers' chav radar will stop them from coming within 20 feet of the place.

ⓒ Mon–Sat, 8pm–2am

ⓙ £9.50

## Las Iguanas

Greek Street
(0113) 243 9533

You still remember that one-horse town in Chile which turned into the fiesta of a lifetime, or the bar in Copacabana where you danced 'til dawn with a dusky Hispanic beauty? The people at Las Iguanas can't bring back the glory days (sadly, nothing can, short of a crazy scientist, Michael J Fox and a Delorean travelling at 88 miles an hour) but they can bring just a little bit of that Latino spirit to darkest Leeds. Sup on a sugary caipirinha, wiggle to the hip-shaking salsa, grab yourself a bite to eat and keep an eye out for that Copacabana girl.

ⓒ Mon–Thu, 12pm–11pm; Fri–Sat, 12pm–11.30pm; Sun, 12pm–10.30pm

ⓙ £11.50

## If Bar

44–48 The Headrow
(0113) 245 2575

Stuff raising money for the church roof fund, we've found a much more deserving cause. The poor folk at Life Bar are so skint they can't afford to replace the 'L' and the 'E' that seem to have been stolen from the sign above their door. So get yourselves down there and donate some of your hard-earned cash. In return, with a restaurant, bar and club you could easily eat, drink, dance and, if you've worked hard enough during the five to nine happy hour, sleep there.

ⓒ Mon, 11am–2am; Tue & Wed, 11am–11.30pm; Thu & Sat, 11am–2am; Sun, 12pm–12.30am; Food, Mon–Sun, 11am–9.30pm

ⓘ Pork fillets, £8.50

ⓙ £9.95

# Drink

## Mamyle

**70–72 New Briggate**

**(07821) 415 050**

A relaxed and funky bar in Leeds's classy Northern Quarter. As well as showcasing DJs playing hip-hop, R'n'B and soul on Friday and Saturday nights, this place also allows people to stick on tunes from their own CDs, MP3s or iPods. So, by all means, take down MC Hammer's *Greatest Hits*. We can't guarantee that it'll get played or, for that matter, that the rest of the punters won't attempt to stone you to death with dry-roasted peanuts. But if you take down your finest pair of Hammer trousers and do the dance, with all the flailing material, you'll at least be hard to hit.

☻ Sun–Thu, 6pm–1am; Fri–Sat, 6pm–2am

✪ £10.50

## Milo

**10 Call Lane**

**(0113) 245 7101**

Oh my God I can't believe it, Ricky from the Kaiser Chiefs used to work here before he packed up his eyeline and left to become a full-time rock star. This ultra-cool, ultra-small bar offers DJ nights, a laid-back atmosphere and reasonably priced drinks. So why not go down, buy yourself a pint and reminisce about that time Ricky asked you out. Well okay, he didn't ask you out exactly but he definitely winked at you. Don't listen to her. He didn't have something in his eye. Jealousy is a terrible thing.

☻ Tue–Sat, 5pm–2am; Food, Sat, 1pm–7pm

🍴 Club sandwich, £2.96

✪ £9.95

## Mook

**Hirst's Yard**

**(0113) 245 9967**

You've got to hand it to Mook. Despite being situated down a back alley where wheelie bins seem to congregate and having a name that sounds like a sickeningly cute euphemism for female genitalia (or maybe that's just us – the doctor told us we shouldn't have watched *King Kong*), it still manages to maintain a certain level of chic. It's definitely never short of punters. Of course that may have more than a little to do with the outstanding cocktail list and the 2-4-1 happy hour.

☻ Sun–Thu, 4pm–12am & 1am; Fri–Sat, 12pm–2am; Happy hour, Sun–Mon, all day; Tue–Sat, 4pm–8pm

✪ £8.50

## Oracle

**3 Brewery Place**

**(0113) 246 9912**

Looking for an alternative to Greek Street and Call Lane? Well, look no further, because Oracle is an award-winning bar/restaurant. The food hinges around some really great value gourmet burgers, all for under six pounds. The bar's stunning location overlooking the river is also perfect for sipping one of their sophisticated cocktails. There are two floors available for your dancing delectation: one is open to the public, but the first floor is members only.

◐ *Ground floor, Mon–Sat, 11am–12am;*
*Sun, 10am–10pm; First floor, Mon–Sat,*
*6pm–2am; Sun, 6pm–12.30am*
◑ *The ultimate burger, £5.75*

# Drink

## Prohibition
**Greek Street**
**(0113) 224 0005**

This place laughs in the face of all those straight-laced loonies who demonise the social lubricant that is alcohol. Come down here to worship at the altar of the liquid god without whom we would all be tragic virgins at the age of 33. Show your appreciation by partaking in some of the tastiest cocktails in Leeds. Treat yourself to a Strawberry Jeeves or tickle those taste buds with an Arizona Cooler. A law forbidding alcohol. It makes you shudder just to think of it.

Ⓒ *Mon–Wed, 12pm–12am; Thu, 12pm–1am; Fri–Sat, 12pm–2am; Sun, 12pm–12am; Food, Mon–Sun, 12pm–10pm*

🍴 *Open top steak sandwich, £7.95*

💲 *£10.95*

## Quid Pro Quo
**Yorkshire House, Greek Street**
**(0113) 244 8888**

Now you know damn well that Latin and alcohol don't mix. One too many nights hanging around outside the local offy with a two-litre bottle of cider scuppered your Latin GCSE. Just think where you might be now otherwise: probably conversing with Latinites in sunny Latiny. Oh well, console yourself by drinking copious amounts of wine and ale in this lovely wine and ale bar. Less pretentious than its neighbours, so you shouldn't bump into anyone speaking Latin which, let's face it, would only depress you.

Ⓒ *Mon–Wed, 12pm–11pm; Thu–Sat, 12pm–2am; Food, Mon–Sun, 12pm–8pm*

🍴 *Homemade burgers, £5*

💲 *£10.50*

## The Reform
**12 Merrion Street**
**(0113) 244 4080**

You wake up and immediately regret it. Half-drowned memories swim round your head like goldfish in a bowl. What on earth did you get up to last night? You can't quite remember but you know it won't have been pretty. This is it – it's time to reform. Don't be fooled though. This cracker of a venue is not the place to redeem yourself. In fact with sumptuous leather armchairs, a bar stocked with continental beer and some eclectic rock'n'roll sounds you'll be back dancing on the table with your underpants on your head before you can say Alcoholics Anonymous.

Ⓒ *Mon–Sat, 5pm–2am*

💲 *£11.90*

## Revolution
48 Call Lane
(0113) 243 2778

You and your mate are still arguing about which of you is the baddest mo'fo in Headingley. You've tried to settle it with a thumb war and a farting competition, but so far it's a draw. There's only one thing for it: a vodka-drinking contest at Revolution. Start off gently with a bubblegum-flavoured shot and gradually work your way up to the dreaded chilli vodka. By the next morning, you'll have no taste buds left and no memory of who was victorious, so you'll probably have to do it all over again. Shame.

🕒 Mon–Sat, 12pm–2am; Sun, 1pm–12.30am; Food, Mon–Sun, 12pm–6pm
🍴 Chicken baguette, £5.50
💷 £9.50

## Sandinista
Cross Belgrave Street
(0113) 305 0372

If you're not one to take five hours to get ready only to go out and look bored, Sandinista could be for you. No one cares how you look. This bar attracts a mixed bag of people, but the music unites them: rock'n'roll, pop, glam and indie. On the play list everyone from Bowie to Mylo to The Darkness (complete with air guitar homage). A perfect after-dinner drinks compliment to the Reliance and just a hop, skip and a pogo away.

🕒 Mon–Tue, 12pm–12am; Wed–Thu, 12pm–1am; Fri–Sat, 12pm–2am; Sun, 12pm–12.30am
🍴 Piccadillo, £5.50
💷 £11

## Revolution Electric Press
41 Cookridge Street, Millennium Square
(0113) 380 4992

This place likes to think of itself as the cool urban centre of Leeds. And as the city goes, it's a pretty top venue. If you fancy an afternoon drink near Millennium Square, or if you plan on chilling in some comfortable chairs with your mates over a pint, or two… or five, this place will fit the bill. Enjoy the indoor courtyard and the view of Millennium Square, but don't get absolutely bladdered here, lest the cool and beautiful set frown on you; as they're likely to do when you're waving your hands in the air, singing *Itsy Bitsy Teeny Weeny Yellow Polka Dot Bikini*.

🕒 Mon–Sat, 12pm–2am; Sun, 1pm–12.30am
💷 £8.00

# Drink

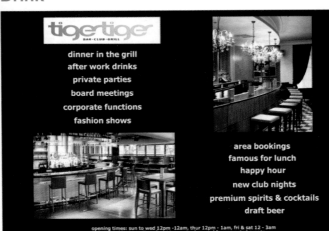

## Tiger Tiger

**The Light, 117 Albion Street**

**(0113) 236 6999**

If you don't fancy the Otley Run because there are hail stones the size of tennis balls falling from the sky, or, in the case of you southerners, because there's a light drizzle, you can still do a mini pub crawl without having to venture into the great outdoors. In Tiger Tiger you can stumble happily from the lounge to the Moroccan kaz bar to the main bar without giving a second thought to the storm raging outside. Until chucking out time that is, when you probably won't be able to get a taxi for love nor money.

ⓒ *Mon–Sat, 11am–2am; Sun, 12pm–12am; Food, Mon–Sun, 12am–5pm & 5pm–late (separate menus)*

## The Wardrobe

**6 St Peters Building, St Peters Square**
**(0113) 383 8800**

Probably not the wisest place for the old 'I'll have a shot of everything on the shelf barman – just fill up this pint glass for me'. Wearing its heart on its sleeve, the first thing you notice as you walk into the Wardrobe is the massive number of bottles behind its bar. If you do decide to hit the spirits though, beware: there's a large concave mirror on the wall by the entrance to the club which can become quite disturbing to eyes twisted by ruinous amounts of the hard stuff.

Ⓒ *Mon–Wed, 12pm–1am; Thu–Sat, 12pm–2am; Food, 9am–10pm*
Ⓘ *Tomato and basil risotto, £6*
Ⓐ *£14*

---

## PUBS

## Adelphi

**3–5 Hunslet Road**
**(0113) 245 6377**

It's a rather bleak fact of life that in most Leeds pubs you'll struggle to find a decent pint of John Smith's. Fortunately though, The Adelphi will serve you a pint of the cleanest, tastiest ale in Yorkshire, and it could hardly be fresher, since they're next to the brewery. They've got all kinds of stuff on the go to keep you entertained, with a craft night on Sundays (the mind boggles), a quiz night and comedy too. Cheap, solid pub grub and decent live music nights make this the kind of place our great county was built on.

Ⓒ *Sun–Wed, 12pm–11pm;*
*Thu–Sat, 12pm–12am*

# Drink

## Bar Censsa

31 Boar Lane

(0113) 244 5220

Your train's been cancelled due to a rather strong gust of wind and you have a couple of hours to kill before the next one arrives. Out of the corner of your eye you spot a bloke muttering to himself and twitching violently. Bitter experience has taught you that you attract such characters like an industrial-strength magnet, so you hurry off in search of a convenient pub. Snappy service, fab food and a chilled atmosphere make Bar Censsa just the place for a quick pit stop. Just make sure you don't lose track of time. This place isn't open all night and Twitchy the Tramp is still lurking.

 *Mon–Wed, 7am–12am; Thu–Sat, 7am–2am; Sun, 11am–10.30pm*

## Barracuda

20 Woodhouse Lane

(0113) 244 1212

From the outside, this South African sports bar looks like a branch of Pound-Stretcher and although you may be disappointed to find you can't buy a complete Royal Doulton tea service for a quid, Barracuda does offer extremely cheap beer. In fact this is exactly the place to come and watch some quality World Cup action. Just make sure you get here in plenty of time to bag one of those booths with a screen right next to the table. That way no one will notice you crying like a baby when England lose on penalties to the Germans.

 *Mon–Wed, 11am–11pm; Thu, 11am–12am; Fri–Sat 11am–2am; Sun, 12pm–11pm. Food, Mon–Sat, 11am–6pm; Sun, 12pm–6pm*

## Beckett's Bank

28–30 Park Row

(0113) 394 5900

You might stand out a bit in Beckett's Bank if you have a symmetrical face. Most of the regulars seem to divide their drinking time between this place and the local park bench. The rest are apparently escapees from a nearby loony bin. Or maybe that bloke who stumbled over to share his life story isn't a complete fruitcake and actually is the creative genius behind *Danger Mouse*. Anyway, you know what to expect when you go to a Wetherspoons pub. The fact is you can drink enough to anaesthetise a small rhinoceros and still have change from 50p.

 *Mon–Sat, 10am–11pm; Sun, 10am–10.30pm; Food, all day until an hour before closing*

## Deer Park

**68 Street Lane**
**(0113) 246 3090**

The Deer Park, or 'The Dear Pint' as Leeds's answer to Oscar Wilde once christened it isn't cheap but then it is in the exclusive little hamlet of Chapel Allerton. The prices have to be kept high to prevent the riff-raff drifting in, which quite frankly would be just beastly. After all, who would want to drink in the kind of uncivilised establishment that allowed people without a black Amex card in? Go down and enjoy a pint for the price of a small terraced house and if you're lucky you might even sneak a glimpse of Jimmy Saville on his way for a pizza. Now then, now then….

◉ *Mon–Sat, 12pm–11pm; Sun, 12pm–10.30pm*

## The Eldon

**90 Woodhouse Lane**
**(0113) 245 3591**

A traditional boozer within spitting distance of the university. They provide good food, a wide selection of beers, lager and a big screen for all the major sporting events. They claim they are busiest from 5pm onwards 'when students finish their lectures'. Yeah, right. Like students actually spend any time at university. They stagger into The Eldon around tea-time because they started the Otley run as soon as the pubs opened. Honestly some people are so naïve. Still, whatever the time, they got the fact that it's rammed with students right. Which is hardly surprising given that it's a pub.

◉ *Mon–Sat, 12pm–11pm; Sun, 12pm–10.30pm*

## Drydock

**Woodhouse Lane**
**(0113) 203 1841**

Drydock is part of the 'Scream' chain, with Munch's missing masterpiece emblazoned all over the place. Why the brains behind these pubs think such a horrific image will inspire fun and frivolity is anyone's guess. But just when you thought things couldn't get any more hilarious, there's a twist. This pub is actually an old boat. Shiver me timbers, that's wacky. Seasickness and 'man overboard' gags are seemingly compulsory amongst the largely student clientele. The top deck is a great place to spend a summer's day, but make sure you get your hands on a yellow card first.

◉ *Mon–Sat, 12pm–1am; Sun, 12pm–12am; Food, Mon–Sun, 12pm–6pm*

# Drink

## The Fenton
**Woodhouse Lane**
**(0113) 245 3908**

This is how a pub should be: dark and dingy, with smoke so thick that unless you're a regular, you'll have no idea where to find the bar. The Fenton has a diverse range of customers. In the corner is a sozzled lecturer, guzzling claret as he marks papers with less and less interest. In the pool room are polite middle-class kids, rebelling against their parents by sporting Nu Metal fashions. Sadly, the BBC has moved, so the orange-faced Christa Akroyd and wacky weatherman are now rarely seen here. Nevertheless, a great British boozer.

Ⓔ *Fri–Sat, 12pm–11pm; Sun, 12pm–10.30pm; Food, Mon–Thu, 11.30am–7pm; Fri–Sat, 12pm–4pm*

## The Grove
**Back Row**
**(0113) 243 9254**

Not a theme pub dedicated to the TV programme that kick-started the careers of everyone's favourite Geordie duo, but one of the finest traditional boozers in Leeds. Refusing to bow down to the faceless new buildings that are sprouting up all over town, the Grove stands defiantly against a backdrop of office blocks and trendy flats. With good beer, friendly staff and salt-of-the-earth drinkers, you can sit around all day and argue to your heart's content about whether it's Ant or Dec who suffers from the affliction of a large spam

Ⓔ *Mon–Sat, 12pm–11pm; Sun, 12pm–10.30pm; Food, Mon–Fri, 12pm–2pm; Sun, 1pm–3pm*

## Headingley Taps
**North Lane**
**(0113) 220 0931**

The Taps is like an inverted tardis. It appears huge as you approach it, but when you step inside, the walls seem to draw in and you're left with about a quarter of the space you expected. Mind you, it's still big enough to handle a moderate gang and is consistently popular with the local students. This may well be down to the fact that they offer classic pub lunches in obscenely huge portions and keep a running speed-eating competition. If you're quick enough to scoff the king size portion in record time you could end up bagging yourself a gallon of beer

Ⓔ *Mon–Sat, 11am–11pm; Sun, 12pm–10.30pm; Food, 2pm–7pm*

## Hyde Park Social Club
**Ash Grove**
(0113) 293 0109

You pop some bread into the toaster because you can't be arsed cooking anything more adventurous for tea; you've got Neighbours to watch after all. Suddenly you become aware of a funny smell. Then all the lights go out. Brilliant, another slug has crawled into the toaster and now the little blighter has gone and fused the whole house. Bloody student accommodation. You consider fixing it, but then you decide that's what housemates are for. So instead you pop down to the Hyde Park Social Club to enjoy a gallon or two of the cheapest beer in Leeds. It's not easy being a student.

🕒 *Mon–Fri, 3.30pm–11pm; Sat, 2pm–11pm; Sun, 2pm–10.30pm*

## Joseph's Well
**Chorley Lane**
(0113) 203 1861

Joseph may be well but some of the regulars in here look decidedly ropey. Still, if you can manage to avoid the less savoury-looking punters, this place is well worth rocking up to, as they put on some cracking live gigs. Try not to get too drunk, though. You'll only get all maudlin when you think about where you might be now if only you'd kept up those guitar lessons and practised harder. Stadium tours, groupies, universal adulation. But let's face it, you'd never have made it to the top with a face like that. (Miaooww.)

🕒 *Mon–Fri, 12pm–12am; Sat, 5pm–12am; Sun, 12pm–10.30pm; Food, Mon–Sun, 12pm–2pm*

## The Library
**229 Woodhouse Lane**
(0113) 244 0794

Aha! Do you see what they've done? They've built a pub right next to the university and they've called it the Library. This means you can tell your poor old dad, who spent thirty years down the pit, breaking his back shovelling coal just so you could reap the benefits of a university education, that you've been hard at it in the Library all day. Absolutely hilarious. Seriously, put that pint down. You should be ashamed of yourself. At least have the decency to tuck a text book under your arm on the way in and use it to prop up the table later.

🕒 *Mon–Sat, 12pm–11pm; Sun, 12pm–10.30pm; Food, Mon–Sun, 12pm–5pm*

# Drink

## The New Inn

68 Otley Road

(0113) 224 9131

Headingley can get depressing sometimes. You often can get the impression you've somehow stumbled into an episode of Hollyoaks, minus the alarming mortality rate. If you just fancy a quiet pint or two, without feeling the need to splash out on cosmetic surgery, why not head down to Far Headingley and sample the humble charms of the New Inn? It's a small pub with a homely feel, which manages to be traditional without the usual horse brass nonsense. There's cheap, unfussy food to be had, all the football on Sky, as well as a pool table. Some of the customers even have jobs.

ⓒ *Mon–Sat, 12pm–11pm; Sun, 12pm–10.30pm; Food, Mon–Sun, 12pm–2.30pm*

## O'Neill's

26 Great George Street

(0113) 244 0810

When great swarms of Irish folk arrived in England in search of the craic and a fresh supply of potatoes, they brought with them some fantastic pubs. Unfortunately O'Neill's just isn't one of them. It's no really bad. You can enjoy four-pint pitchers of Carling for £7.95 while you watch the big game. It just seems to lack a bit of energy and atmosphere It's also full to burst with oirish tat Saying that, it's in a great location because when the footy's finished you can always nip next door to the Vic

ⓒ *Mon–Thu, 12pm–11pm; Fri–Sat, 12pm–12am; Sun, 12pm–10.30pm; Food, daily, 12pm–7pm*

## Original Oak

2 Otley Road

(0113) 275 1322

On a sunny day when there's a test match on in Headingley, there is no better place in the world to be. And you don't have to understand what the hell 'silly mid-off' means to be able to enjoy it. Once play has finished, the pubs fill up and the real fun begins. There's a carnival atmosphere, with people in fancy dress stumbling into Otley Road and being mangled by articulated lorries. You'll have a whale of a time wherever you go. But the place to be has got to be the Original Oak's beer garden. Sixteen Santas, Fred Flintstone and an ostrich can't be wrong

ⓒ *Mon–Sat, 12pm–11pm; Sun, 12pm–10.30pm;*

## Oxygen

15 The Headrow
(0113) 245 8153

Did you know oxygen was invented by a Leeds lad? Well, all the best things come from oop north, like the Beatles, gravy and Leeds United fans. What did southerners ever give us? We'll tell you what – Gary Glitter, jellied eels and Man U supporters. So, we've finally named a pub in honour of Joseph Priestley and his remarkable discovery which, let's face it, has made breathing so much easier. Ok, so this place is actually called Oxygen because it's a non-smoking bar. It's still worth a gander, with its stylish décor and brilliant value food.

🕐 *Mon–Wed, 12pm–12am; Thu–Sat, 12pm–2am; Sun, 12pm–10.30pm*

## The Packhorse

08 Woodhouse Lane
(0113) 245 3980

Ah, the dear old Packhorse may well be of an age when the knacker's yard beckons, but pat her on the head from time to time and she'll happily reward you with a frothy pint of bitter and a smile from the busty barmaid. It's also the local for Boy George's cousin, who will always pose for pics in his 15 minutes of fame. Apart from these simple pleasures, they've also got a cosy pool room (mind the windows when you cue up) a legendary jukebox and an upstairs section, which just doesn't have the same lunatic charm as the floor below.

🕐 *Mon–Sat, 12pm–11pm; Sun, 12pm–10.30pm; Food, Mon–Sun, 12pm–7pm*

## Roundhay Fox

Princes Avenue, Roundhay
(0113) 246 3090

After a gentle stroll through Roundhay Park, it's always nice to regain any calories you've carelessly misplaced by stopping here for a quick drink and a bite to eat. Open fires, exposed beams and cosy little alcoves make for a welcoming atmosphere. And although the price of a glass of wine might well bring a tear to your eye, the food is great value for money and the portions are huge. The fish and chips are especially impressive. Jesus didn't perform a miracle at the feeding of the five thousand. He just got his fish from the same supplier that they use here.

🕐 *Mon–Sat, 12pm–11pm; Sun, 12pm–10.30pm*

# Drink

## The Royal Park
Queens Road
(0113) 275 7494

If all that studying is getting you down why not pop into the Royal Park and learn how to make a living as a pool shark. How hard can it be? They've got a million and six tables so you shouldn't find you have to wait long to commence your training. And if the white ball flies off the table when you're attempting to impress the good-looking barmaid, only to break the nose of that scary looking-bloke covered in tattoos, you can always run down and hide among the gig-goers in the dingy basement.

◉ *Mon–Sat, 12pm–11pm; Sun, 12pm–10.30pm; Food, Mon–Fri, 5pm–8pm; Sat–Sun, 12pm–4pm & 5pm–8pm*

## The Skyrack
2 Otley Road
(0113) 278 1519

Leeds knows a thing or two about local rivalries, as Manchester United and the Bradford Bulls will attest – but they come no fiercer than the duel between the Oak and the Rack. The Oak has a natural advantage (best beer garden in Leeds). The 'Rack has concentrated on packing in the crowds. In terms of popularity, you can't fit a cigarette paper between them. If these pubs had a fight, the Skyrack would be the mouthy skinny lad starting the trouble after one too many shandies. The Original Oak would knock him out with a left hook to the jaw.

◉ *Mon–Tue, 11am–11pm; Wed–Sat, 11am–12.30am; Sun, 12pm–12.30am; Food, 12pm–7pm*

## Stick or Twist
Merrion Street
(0113) 234 9748

This is the pub to go to when you're feeling bad about things. If the outbreak of acne you're suffering from seems particularly cruel considering you're plummeting towards 30, then come here for a few pints and bask in the glow of being the youngest and best looking person in the building. Obviously, this is not an ideal pub to pull in (well, unless you gets your kicks from the toothless types). But it's great for drinking copious amounts of cheap beer and scoffing the famously good value food. Be warned, it gets particularly busy on giro day.

◉ *Mon–Sun, 10am–11pm; Food, daily, until an hour before closing*

□□■□□□□□□□□□

## The Three Horseshoes
**8 Otley Road**
**(0113) 275 7222**

Students are always moaning about paying back their tuition fees, but none of them actually seem to be skint. Your average student these days wears nothing but Yves St Laurent, spends hours on the sun bed, drinks spritzers and that's just the blokes. If there are still any brassick students out here though, this is the pub for you. It's the cheapest place to drink in Headingley, unless you're willing to share bench space with a tramp. The food's good value too. If they embrace 24-hour opening, it'll be a better place to live than student halls.

*Mon–Sat, 12pm–11pm; Sun, 12pm–10.30pm; Food, Mon–Fri, 12pm–8pm; Sun, 12pm–4pm*

## The Victoria Inn
**Great George Street**
**(0113) 246 1386**

Sometimes you hanker after a drink that doesn't have an olive in it and won't set you back four quid. You don't want a big plasma screen, a DJ and bar staff so attractive that you feel obliged to put a bag over your head. There's none of that muck here. Just a bar and some chairs. A great place to get drunk, talk bollocks, sleep it off in the corner and repeat. Forget Churchill, the empire, the monarchy, cloth caps, the 66 World Cup, Shakespeare, the PG Tip chimps and Barbara Windsor: pubs like this are what made Britain great.

*Mon–Sat, 11.30am–11pm; Sun, closed; Food, Mon–Sat, 12pm–7pm*

## Walkabout
**Cookridge Street**
**(0113) 205 6500**

Our proud nation once had a wonderful system for dealing with criminals, whereby we sent them off to a distant shore, waited a couple of hundred years and then started importing their soap operas. The drawback to this system was that we also became inundated with Australian theme bars. The Walkabout chain is the market leader in this cultural phenomenon. Go there for a ripper time, drink a few tinnies and maybe bag yourself a real spunk. In reality, ask yourself why you want to drink in a bar paying homage to the country that gave us Jonno Coleman.

*Mon, 11am–11pm; Tue, 11am–12am; Thu, 11am–1am; Wed & Fri-Sat, 11am–2am*

# Drink

## Wetherspoons

**Leeds City Station, City Square**

**(0113) 247 1676**

This place is the sole reason for missing your train and coming into work hung over for the fourth day on the trot. Wetherspoons certainly isn't shy about advertising its cheap drink deals to tempt you in after a shite day at the office. There's a persistent rumour that they're keen to offer 24-hour drinking as well. Will it happen? Will you ever get to work again? It's probably best not to think about it and just order another pint, or shooter or cocktail jug or two meals for a fiver. Ten quid goes a long way.

ℂ *Mon–Fri, 7.30am–11pm; Sat, 9am–11pm; Sun, 10am–10.30pm; Food, daily, until an hour before closing*

## Whitelocks

**Turks Head Yard (off Briggate)**

**(0113) 245 3950**

Whitelocks is famously Leeds' oldest pub, the first pints pulled in here being enjoyed by John the Baptist and Captain Caveman. Enter this pub on any midweek lunchtime and you'll see a wonderful sight: a crowd of tipsy OAPs, who seemingly have their pension cheques delivered straight into the landlord's cash register. The interior of the pub is reminiscent of Nicholas Lyndhurst's head, the dimensions being very long and thin, which means it can get crowded. But who cares when the beer and food are this good?

ℂ *Mon–Sat, 12pm–11pm; Sun, 12pm–10.30pm; Food, Mon–Sun, 12pm–7pm*

## Woodies

**104 Otley Road**

**(0113) 2784 393**

This is the pub they go to in *Fat Friends*. If you manage to come down when the windows haven't been blacked out to prevent us mere mortals from sneaking a peak at such acting greats as Lisa Riley, this is a fab place to enjoy a few quiet beers, play a bit of pool or watch the footy. We're kinda hoping it becomes a bit of a Mecca for the Weightwatchers crew. It can get a bit busy when they hold the pub quizzes but we wouldn't recommend coming down then anyway. You wouldn't want your mates to find out that you think Fidel Castro plays for Real Madrid.

ℂ *Mon–Sat, 12pm–11pm; Sun, 12pm–10.30pm; Food, Mon–Sat, 12pm–2pm*

# CHAT-UP LINES

THANKS TO ITCHY, YOU NEVER HAVE TO GO HOME ALONE. HOWEVER, PLEASE BE AWARE THAT WE TAKE NO RESPONSIBILITY FOR YOUR ACTIONS AFTERWARDS.

'The word of the day is "legs". Let's go back to my place and spread the word.'

'Your eyes are like spanners... every time you look at me my nuts tighten.'

Break a bit of ice on the bar and say, 'Now I've broken the ice can I buy you a drink?'

'You remind me of a parking ticket. Because you've got "fine" written all over you.'

'Are you wearing mirrored pants? (They say no.) Funny, because I can see myself in them.'

– 'Hi, I'm Mr Right. Someone said you were looking for me.'

– 'What's the name of that hot, black drink they sell in Starbucks?' (They reply, 'Coffee'). 'Sure. Your place or mine?'

– 'Will you help me find my lost puppy? I think he just went into a cheap hotel room over the road.'

– 'Do you like animals? Because I'm a real wildcat when you get to know me.'

– 'Have you just farted? Because you've blown me away.'

– 'I'm no Fred Flintstone, but I can sure make your bed rock.'

– 'Shag me if I'm wrong, but haven't we met before?'

– 'Do you play the trumpet? Only you're making me horny.'

Illustration by Ben Anderson-Bauer

# Dance

# Dance

## CLUBS

### Atrium
**6–9 The Grand Arcade**
**(0113) 242 6116**

Apparently, internet dating sites are full of men claiming they spend their spare time adopting orphans, saving the planet and learning how to salsa. Listening to the odd Ricky Martin song and throwing a few shapes in front of your bedroom mirror does not a salsa dancer make. If you fancy working on your rhythm for real, Atrium hosts a decent Latin night. If not, they have three floors offering an eclectic mix of jazz funk, R'n'B and house.

 ☺ *Mon–Thu, 9pm–2am; Fri, 8.30pm–3am; Sat, 10am–3am*

 ☻ *£4–£6*

### Baja Beach Club
**43a Woodhouse Lane**
**(0113) 245 4088**

Can't afford to go on holiday this year? Well, head on down to Baja Beach instead. It's got all the ingredients for a great summer holiday and you don't even have to leave Leeds. There are semi-naked bar staff, all your mates making tits of themselves on the dance floor and a great big plastic shark. Dance the night away to cheesy muzak and before you know where you are, you'll find yourself waking up in the gutter cuddling a half-eaten kebab. It's because of nights like these that you can't afford to go abroad.

 ☺ *Mon & Wed–Thu, 9pm–2am; Tue, 9.30pm–2.30am; Fri–Sat, 8pm–2.30am; Sun, 9pm–1am*

 ☻ *Free–£5*

### Bar Phono
**16 The Merrion Centre**
**(0113) 242 9222**

Joe Strummer once livened things up here by busking in the queue. Even though he's been dead a while, we reckon he'd still spice things up. Open practically every night of the week, Phono is a stalwart of Leeds's alternative scene. Marc Almond used to DJ here and the Goth Two-Step is supposed to have been invented within these very walls. Regulars are fiercely loyal to this little club. 'Oblivion' on Saturdays is definitely worth checking out. And why is it called 'Oblivion'? We reckon that might have something to do with the fact that they sell vodka and coke for a quid.

 ☺ *Wed, 10pm–2am; Thu, 10pm–2am; Fri & Sat, 9.30pm–2.30am; Sun, 7pm–12am*

□□□□■□□□□□□□

## The Bassment

**Wade Lane, Merrion Centre**
**(0113) 245 0689**

The Bassment, owned by the same guys who own Bar Phono round the corner, is famed for its Goth and 'Rock of Ages' nights. This club consists of a single room where your feet will stick to the floor and you can get Tizer on tap; features which may not be entirely unconnected. Don't be alarmed if you come face to face with a chap dressed head-to-toe in tin foil, kohl, spikes, chains and rubber. You'll find he's as harmless as your Christmas turkey (and we're not referring that year that your mum failed to defrost it properly).

◉ Thu, 10pm–2am; Fri, 10pm–3am; Sat, 9pm–2.30am

## Bondi Beach Bar

**Queens Buildings, City Square**
**(0113) 243 4733**

Bondi is home to Leeds's only revolving dance floor. You can see where they were going with this: a load of people already off their faces on cocktails, spinning. Why other nightclubs haven't followed in their footsteps is anyone's guess. When this place is busy it gets unbelievably hot, and you run a high risk of melting or vaporising. If you manage to avoid both of these pitfalls, get yourself on that famous dance floor where the opportunities for projectile vomit-related fun are endless. *'I'm spinning around, move out my way...'*

◉ Mon–Sat, 5pm–2.30am; Sun, 5pm–10.30pm
🎟 £2–5

## The HiFi Club 2 Central Road Leeds LS1 6DE
### The North's Premier Funk, Soul, Jazz & Live Music Venue

# Dance

### The Elbow Room
**64 Call Lane**
**(0113) 245 7011**

Don't be put off by the student-union style entrance, because The Elbow Room should be part of any self-respecting night out, whether you want to dance, shoot pool, eat, drink or ogle the lovely Leeds talent. There's everything here you could possibly desire. Ok, maybe not everything, but there are 15 pool tables, two bars, a dance floor, great music and food served 'til late. The Sugar Beat Club on Saturdays is definitely worth a look. A word of warning though: trying that leg-in-the-air trick shot at 3am while balancing your ice cream cocktail on the table is only going to end in tears.

**☉** *Mon–Sat, 12pm–2am; Sun, 2pm–10.30am*
**☎** £6–£7

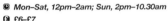

# Evolution

**Cardigan Fields Leisure Centre, Kirkstall**
**(0113) 263 2632**

Any club which manages to pull in the entire student population of Leeds on a Saturday night is worth checking out. It's well out of town, so you can behave shamelessly without fear of reprisals. The only people to witness you getting your tits out on stage will all have been too shedded to be able to remember the next morning. Although, as The Streets carp on their single, with the growing popularity of camera phones, you may have to think twice about the snap-happy mob before risking any seriously outrageous behaviour.

🕐 *Mon–Thu, 10pm–2am; Sat, 10pm–3am*
💷 *£3–5*

# The Fruit Cupboard

**0–52 Call Lane**
**(0113) 243 8666**

The Fruit Cupboard is aptly named; partly because of its firm and fruity clientele and partly because it's the size of a cupboard. Affectionately known as 'The Fight Cupboard' among some of Leeds's wittier residents, you have to pick your nights carefully here. Despite being located on trendy Call Lane, this place is a world away from the fashionistas in brb, which, let's face it, is not necessarily a bad thing. Playing the best of R'n'B and hip-hop you can enjoy a top night of gettin' yer freak on. Just be careful who you spill your pint over.

🕐 *Mon, 9.30pm–2.30am; Tue, 10pm–2.30am; Wed–Fri, 10pm–late; Sat, 10.30pm–4am*
💷 *80p–£8*

# Flares

**40 Boar Lane**
**(0113) 205 1931**

Yeah, baby, yeah! Dust down that white jump suit, practise a few of your John Travolta moves in front of your bedroom mirror (God, yes, you've still got it) and boogie on down to Flares. The 70s revival is an acquired taste, a bit like decking our house out like the Blackpool Illuminations or stone-cladding. Here, with the sounds of Abba and the Bee Gees ringing in your ears, you can get down on the dance floor and pay homage to an altogether simpler time when dress sense and Jade Goody were yet to be invented.

🕐 *Mon–Wed, 8pm–12am; Thu, 8pm–1am; Fri–Sat, 7pm–2am; Sun, 7pm–12am*
🎟 *Free–£3*

## HiFi

2 Central Road
(0113) 242 7353

A stalwart player on the Leeds scene, HiFi hasn't missed a trick. Playing a staple diet of funk, soul, R'n'B and Motown (which for once doesn't just mean *Superstition* breaking up Ja Rule and Destiny's Child), HiFi also offers regular gigs, alternative nights, comedy and amazing Sunday lunches, complete with live jazz and papers. You might be able to tell by now that they pay attention to even the smallest detail, so this venue is constantly rammed. It still feels like your own little secret.

🕒 Mon–Wed, 10pm–2am; Thu, 10pm–2.30am; Fri, 10pm–3am; Sat, 10pm–3am (comedy nights 7pm); Sun, 12pm–12.30am

💷 £3–£6

## MPV

4–8 Church Street
(0113) 243 9486

Quite a peculiar place this; if you don't know what you're looking for you'll probably walk straight past the four large red pods wedged under the railway arches. During the day they resemble a group of Transformers (robots in disguise, not something you'd find in a nuclear power plant). And the similarity doesn't end there. At night they flip a few bits up and out and suddenly they become something very different entirely. In this case it's a hip and groovy nightspot and not a huge lorry, but it's so cool, we're sure even Megatron would approve.

🕒 Thu–Sat, 10pm–2.30am

💷 Free

## The Northern Light

Cross York Street
(0113) 243 6446

Classy, chic and stylish. That's the name of the game here. A former school house that's been smoothly transformed into a smart combination of a restaurant, bar and club. Two rooms of soulful, uplifting housey-type beats provide the soundtrack to a cracking vibe which pulls in a funky clientele. All this changes though on hard house nights, where if you don't go in armed with a Burberry baseball cap and Henry Lloyd all-in-one bodysuit, you'll stick out like a green donkey on a bus.

🕒 Mon–Sat, 9pm–2am (term time);
Thu–Sat, 9pm–2am (out of term time)

💷 Prices vary

# Dance

## The Wardrobe
### 6 St Peter's Building
### (0113) 383 880

This is a classic drinks-after-work venue, so although you can expect a huge influx of suits undoing their ties and talking loudly about office politics just after the 5 o'clock turf-out, at some point they slope off home to eat their teas in front of the telly, and the mood lifts as the evening draws in. The downstairs club has a bar stocked with pretty much every spirit produced since distillation took off and all at reasonable prices. With a fantastic selection of live acts, DJs and unique club nights on offer, you will never again have an excuse for finding yourself in Heaven and Hell again.

*Mon–Fri, 9am–1am; Sat, 12pm–1am*
*Prices vary*

## Wire
### 2–8 Call Lane
### (0113) 243 1481

Yet another cracking new nightclub, no that Leeds is lacking. Brought to you by the same people behind the HiF Club, who've also recently revampe the Faversham as a music venue, this place is bound to be a runaway success A massive basement venue, playing indie, rock'n'roll, alternative dance electro and D'n'B, this club will appea to anyone who's serious about the BPMs. If top-notch nightclubs kee opening in this city, you're never going to be in a fit state to go to work. Wav goodbye to that promotion right now

*Wed–Sat, from 10pm–2am*
*Prices vary*

# GET INTO THE GROOVE

'I BET THAT YOU LOOK GOOD ON THE DANCEFLOOR', SING THE ARCTIC MONKEYS.
JUDGING BY THE SHAMBOLIC MOVES ON MOST CITY CENTRE DANCEFLOORS,
THEY LOST THAT BET. FOLLOW THE GUIDE TO SHAKIN' YOUR ASS LIKE ITCHY, AND
PREPARE TO BE THE TALK OF THE TOWN (FOR ALL THE RIGHT REASONS).

*Illustration by Anja Wohlstrom*

**1.**

1. **The Travolta**
   Reach for the sky and reclaim
   this classic from yer dad.
2. **Hand spin**
   Twirl those legs like a castrato.
3. **Step and clap**
   This simple move served Rick
   Astley well in the 80s, so nick
   it for the noughties.

**2.**

**3.**

Gay

# Gay

## BARS

### The Base
**24–32 Bridge End**
**(0113) 368 4648**

You can pretty much guarantee that anywhere with an art gallery that pays homage to Mel B doesn't take itself too seriously (and if they do, they really should consider getting help). The Base couldn't be any more at ease with itself if it tried. It's a friendly, unpretentious pub that attracts a varied, up-beat crowd. With cabaret and quiz nights to keep you entertained, a gay old time will be had by all.

Ⓒ Sun–Thu, 12.30pm–12am; Fri–Sat, 4pm–2am; Food, Mon–Fri, 12pm–2pm
Ⓘ Grilled tuna steak salad, £4.95
Ⓐ £8.45

### Blayde's
**Blayde's Yard, Lower Briggate**
**(0113) 244 5590**

With the employees regularly performing dance routines behind the bar, it's like a scene out of *Coyote Ugly* in here, only the people are, well, uglier. That said, it's not every day you get people prepared to make complete fools of themselves in public for nowt, so we probably shouldn't complain. Apart from these moments of spontaneous hip-wiggling, you can expect raucous behaviour and lots of loud lesbians, all crammed into a venue the size of a shoe box; which can only be a good thing.

Ⓒ Mon–Thu, 2pm–11pm; Fri–Sat, 2pm–1am; Sun, 2pm–12.30am
Ⓐ £2.60 (small bottle)

### The Bridge
**Bridge End**
**(0113) 244 4734**

Walking into some venues in Leeds feels like you've stumbled into a scene from a Western. The bar falls silent, tumbleweed blow down the street behind you, and everyone turns and looks you up and down to ascertain whether you are cool enough to be allowed to drink in their company. Thankfully, this place is nothing like that. A word of warning though: Thursday night is karaoke night, so brace yourself for 38 different versions of Gloria Gaynor's anthem *I Will Survive*. Bring your own ear plugs.

Ⓒ Mon–Wed, 12pm–12am; Thu, 12pm–1am; Fri–Sat, 12pm–2am; Sun, 1pm–12am
Ⓐ £3.10 (small bottle)

## ibre

8 Lower Briggate
(13) 234 1304

fish tank where only the brightest, most beautiful specimens will survive. The st of us cold-water types, who were probably only won at the fair anyway, can awp at the window before swimming off find somewhere where we won't be fed the sharks if our mullet doesn't have e requisite number of blonde streaks in It's a good job we only have a seven-cond memory, eh? Now, where were e? Oh, yeah. Fibre. A tropical fish tank...

Mon–Wed, 11am–12am; Thu, 11am–1am;
i–Sat, 11am–2am; Sun, 12pm–7pm;
od, Mon–Sun, 12pm–7pm
Oriental duck wrap, £4
£9.50

## ueens Court

Lower Briggate
(13) 245 9449

ey might be the heart of the Leeds gay ene, but where exactly is the soul? QC quite frankly, getting a bit boring. The mosphere is stale and uninviting and ey've also recruited some particularly ncey bar staff. If you do find yourself th nowhere else to go though, you can aw some comfort from the fact that the od is pretty good and reasonably priced. d if you hit the bar at happy hour, the nks are reduced from extortionate to t above average, but we'd recommend ing your time to find more fun elsewhere.

Mon–Sat, 12am–2am; Sun, 12pm–11pm
Mixed grill, £6.95
£7.50

## Velvet

11–12 Hirst's Yard
(0112) 245 5079

If you're not one of the in-crowd, you can expect to be mistaken for a waitress in this bar/restaurant. Velvet is arsey in the extreme and it shows. That said, it's still worth a visit, if you follow our instructions: wait until somebody asks you for the bill, scribble down the first extortionate number that comes into your head and tell them you only take cash. All you have to do then is wait for them to hand over all that lovely moolah. Nice revenge on the cool cats. Then go and have yourself a top night out at Baja Beach.

Ⓢ Mon–Sat, 12pm–12am; Sun, 12pm–10.30pm;
Food, Wed–Sat, 12pm–12am; Sun, 2pm–6pm

# Gay

## CLUBS

### Homo@Mission

8–13 Heaton's Court

(0870) 122 0114

With a friendly, fun-loving ambience and open attitude, Homo is a gay night that welcomes everyone, whether you be gay, straight, bi, tri, animal, vegetable or mineral. They might draw the line at Jeremy Clarkson, but we're not sure. The music mirrors the attitude of the fun-loving clientele, so expect to hear everything from Kylie to Kool and The Gang. It's cheesy, it's camp and it's cheap. What more could you want on a Thursday night? Oh. Well, you might get that here too.

🎧 *Thu, 10pm–3am*

💷 *£3*

### SpeedQueen@ The Warehouse

19–21 Somers Street

(0113) 246 8287

The Leeds club scene is always changing but no one seems to tire of the ever-popular SpeedQueen. Put on an outrageous outfit and dance the night away with some of the most colourful characters in Leeds (and we don't mean that old git who always swears at the bus stop). Make sure you get there early, though, or you may well be sent packing. This place fills up fast, and we wouldn't want you to miss out on the fun. And frankly, you're going to stand out like a grown man at a McFly gig wearing that rubber ensemble in Beckett's Bank.

🎧 *Sat, 10pm–4am*

💷 *£8–£10*

## SHOPS

### Clone Zone

164 Briggate

(0113) 242 6967

One-stop sex shop selling everything for the gay lifestyle. Expect lots of rubber in every size and shape from *Oops, did it again* to *Hit me baby, one more time*. Perhaps not the place to take your gran shopping, but then again, if you can't quite work out how to break the news about your sexual preference, casually leading her into this place might just do the trick. Of course, it could also be the thing that finishes her off. Ah, well. Either way it'll save you having that awkward conversation.

🎧 *Mon–Sat, 11am–7pm; Sun, 12pm–7pm*

# LISTEN UP OMI PALONES!

**THOSE OF YOU OUT CHARPERING FOR A DOLLY DISH WITH A NICE BASKET MIGHT WANT TO TAKE NOTE OF AN IMMINENT LINGUISTIC REVIVAL ON THE UK GAY SCENE.**

Polari, the secret language used by London's 1960s gay community to communicate in public without fear of the law, has long been as dead as a dodo's cassette collection.

But the pink parlance is starting to come back out of the closet. What with a reinvigorated Morrissey being a self-confessed polari user, as well as usage of polari becoming almost compulsory amongst staff at popular London kitsch cabaret venue Madame JoJo's, it looks like pretty soon anyone who's anyone will need to know their fantabuloso lingo.

I'M BONAR FOR THAT OMI PALONE

**'What a cod meese omi'**
– 'What a vile ugly man'

**'Vada the colour of his eyes'**
- 'Check out the size of his penis'

**'Vada the palone with the matini'**
- 'Look, he's gay'

**'I'm bonar for that omi palone'**
- 'I'm attracted to that man'

**'Nice basket'**
- 'Nice trouser bulge'

**'You're joshed up'**
– 'You're looking your best'

**'Aunt Nell!'**
– 'Listen to me!'

**'Vada the cod zhoosh on that omi palone'**
– 'Look at the awful clothes on that man'

**'Nanti vogue near me'**
– 'Don't light that cigarette near me'

**'Let's blag some dishes'**
– 'Let's pick up some good-looking guys'

**'There's nix mungarlee here'**
– 'There's nothing to eat here'.

# Shopping

# Shop

## AREAS

### Briggate and The Arcades

Briggate offers everything a shopper could ever need, all on one long strip of pavement. On a Saturday afternoon it's fun to make like Mel Gibson in *Braveheart* as you stand at the top of the street contemplating the sea of shoppers you are about to do battle with. It's probably best if you don't don the blue and white war paint though. Refuge from the battlefield is available in the beautiful arcades with their marble floors and pillars and those stunning arched glass ceilings. So relax, buy yourself a coffee and take time to ponder one of life's great mysteries: why-oh-why are those plastic men beating seven shades out of that bell?

### Kirkgate Market
Vicar Lane
(0113) 214 5162

You've just spent the last of this month's wage on some of life's little essentials. In this case, you were forced to splash out on a new top and some sexy underwear. You're going to get lucky tonight or make a complete tit of yourself trying. Anyway, now you're skint and you've still got over a week until you next get paid, so you've just about given up on the prospect of being able to eat out then. But what's this, you take a wrong turn at the Corn Exchange and you stumble into the market. This place is a revelation. With these prices you'll be able to eat like a king for the next seven days and all for £1.37.

## SHOPPING CENTRES

### The Corn Exchange
Call Lane
(0113) 234 0363

An industrial-strength magnet to all the teenage goths in Leeds, who hang around outside with faces so sour you'd think they've just received news of plans to criminalise eyeliner. God only knows why they look so miserable; this place is amazing. The Corn Exchange houses some of the best independent shops in town. There are also a couple of cafés where you can relax with your mates and come up with original ways of making one of those doom merchants outside crack a smile. © *Mon–Fri, 10am–5.30pm; Sat, 9.30am–6pm; Sun, 11am–4pm*

## The Light
### The Headrow
**(0113) 218 2060**

Now we all remember from our religious education lessons at school what happened to Saul on the road to Damascus. He saw The Light. And he was so grateful to find an assortment of wonderful shops, restaurants serving delicious food from all corners of the earth, a fully-equipped gym and a 13-screen cinema all in one lovely rain-free setting that he changed his name to Paul and has been thanking the Lord ever since. Next week, we'll be learning about Joseph, and how he managed to make brightly coloured coats fashionable again.

🕐 *Mon–Sat, 9am–6pm; Thu, 9am–8pm & Sun, 11am–5pm*

## House of Fraser
### 140–142 Briggate
**(0113) 243 5235**

Not as posh as Harvey Nics, but at least that means you can go in without donning full evening wear and the sales assistants won't look at you with the kind of contempt usually reserved for somone who's just shot an OAP through the head with a crossbow. There's an excellent range of make up, including old favourites like Elizabeth Arden and contemporary brands, like Benefit and Bobbi Brown. Clothes-wise this place combines chic designers with classy brands like Oasis, CUK and Therapy. Definitely the place to go if you're looking to get your sweaty mitts on some affordable designer jeans.

🕐 *Mon–Wed & Fri, 9am–5.30pm; Thu, 9am–7pm; Sat, 9am–6pm; Sun, 11am–5pm*

## DEPARTMENT STORES

## Harvey Nichols
### 107 Briggate
**(0113) 204 8888**

It's Saturday morning, and your hangover can't face staying at home in front of the box with all those impossibly chirpy kids' TV presenters. So you drag yourself out of bed and head into town to wander round Harvey Nics for a while, fantasising about how wonderful life would be if only you had a few more pounds in your bank and a few less pounds on your big fat arse. Before long, you're ready to head to the pub to mull over the fact that if you drank less, you'd probably be richer and thinner.

🕐 *Mon–Fri, 10am–6pm; Thu–Fri, 10am–7pm; Sat, 9am–7pm; Sun, 11am–5pm*

# Shop

## MENS' CLOTHING

### Aspecto

1 Queen Victoria Street
(0113) 245 0150

You've got to have a lot of faith in the shoes you stock if you just line them up along the perimeter of your ground floor and leave them to sell themselves. Well ok, not entirely by themselves. The Toni and Guy cast-off behind the till makes sure you don't leave without handing over some of your hard-earned dough. If you're after something more than footwear, the jungle-themed basement is full to bursting, sporting Carrhart, G-Star and Evisu street-wear.

◉ *Mon–Sat, 9.30am–6pm;*
*Sun, 9.30am–5pm*

### Ginger Ink

26 Otley Road
(0113) 278 9944

Aha! So this is why the students of Headingley are all beginning to look like they've been cloned from children's TV presenters. It seems they've all been heading down to Ginger Ink for their togs, and for good reason. Top labels, reasonable prices and NUS discounts mean that this place is fast becoming the one-stop fashion shop for lazy, tax-dodging types. Once they're fully kitted out, all that remains to be done is to get a funky new trim up top, then spend the afternoon flirting with a cardboard cut-out of June Sarpong, in between watching old episodes of *Friends*.

◉ *Mon–Sat, 10am–6pm; Sun, 12pm–4pm*

### Olivers

5–7 Queen Victoria Street
(0113) 246 8887

A classic no mess, low-stress shop which focuses on the smarter side of casual. Big names with similarly sized price tags. Everything here is a safe bet, aimed at your classy, suave man-about town. They have service to match – just ask if you need help finding a certain something. A real life-saver if you need to pull out all the stops to impress a lovely lady, or even a lovely lady's parents, if it comes to that. The best thing is that these clothes will look good on you even if the only six-pack you've got is waiting for you in the fridge at home.

◉ *Mon–Sat, 9.30am–5.30pm;*
*Sun, 11am–4pm*

# Shop

## UNISEX CLOTHING

### All Saints

**33–35 Queen Victoria Street**

**(0113) 243 2434**

Cool clothes with an ever-so-slightly blasphemous twist, at prices that aren't exactly cheap, but not at all bad for what you're getting. Their trademark 'Jesus Loves You' belts and 'Mary Is My Homegirl' t-shirts are practically uniform among trendy mulleted types in Leeds, but there are some more original, funky threads to be had as well. You just need to look a little bit harder for them. That said, it's probably not the best place to come if you're looking for an outfit to wear to your nephew's christening.

📀 *Mon–Sat, 9am–6pm; Sun, 12pm–5pm*

### Great Clothes

**4 Berking Avenue**

**(0113) 235 0303**

Just five minutes from the centre of Leeds, this is one of the biggest independent retail outlets in the city. They offer massive discounts on high street and designer wear, as well as free parking and free alterations. There's even a coffee shop where you can leave your fella to pore over the sports pages while you go bargain hunting in peace. When you see yourself in your brand spanking new outfit you might even realise that you can do better than that slab of lard you call a boyfriend and leave him there.

📀 *Mon–Fri, 9.30am–9pm; Sat, 9.30am–*
*pm; Sun, 11am–5pm; Bank Holidays,*
*30am–6pm*

### Exit

**Corn Exchange**

**(0113) 246 9301**

Getting their own back for years of humiliation and degradation at the hands of PG Tips, chimpanzees have launched a range of clothing for humans under the pseudonym Paul Frank. They dress us up, watch us drink copious amounts of alcohol and laugh as we stumble around the streets behaving like complete animals. If being used for their amusement makes you feel uncomfortable, other brands of trainers and skate wear are also available here. Otherwise, remember what we've said the next time you find yourself monkeying around.

📀 *Mon–Sat, 9.30am–5.30pm;*
*Sun, 11am–4.30pm*

# Shop

## WOMENS' CLOTHING

### Aqua
Corn Exchange, Call Lane
(0113) 243 3336

A boutique selling the kind of clothes that make other women stop you in the street and ask you where you bought them. If the women in question are skinnier and better looking than you, smile sweetly and send them along to M&S. Aqua is a tad on the pricey side, but then you get what you pay for. If you need an outfit for that special occasion, their clothes are well worth shelling out a few bob extra for. For the financially disadvantaged, their sale store (also in the Corn Exchange) might be a more viable option.

© *Mon–Sat, 10am–5.30pm; Sun, 12pm–4pm*

### Dawn Stretton
30 Central Road
(0113) 244 9083

Cinderella, you shall go to the ball! In fact, Dawn will ensure even the ugliest sister is dressed to impress the pickiest of princes. With half the cast of Emmerdale, Louise Redknapp and Melinda Messenger often seen strutting about done up in Stretton style, it's clear she's more than used to dressing girls for that big occasion. Definitely safer than relying upon your fairy godmother to provide a frock. After all, you can't put your faith in someone who expects you to ride home in a big orange pumpkin after a night on the sauce

© *Mon–Thu, 9.30am–5.30pm; Fri–Sat, 9.30am–6pm; Sun, 11am–5pm*

### Vicky Martin
42 Victoria Quarter
(0113) 244 1477

Contrary to popular opinion, this shop isn't owned by Ricky's twin sister. Full to the brim of funky, unusual pieces, all of which are perfect for a girl's night out on the town. You might want to give this place a miss until you manage to shed that extra holiday weight though, as the clothes here are definitely designed to make the most of your figure. On the other hand, seeing yourself bursting out of one of their sexy little dresses might be just the incentive you need to get your lazy arse down the gym. After which you can get back to living la vida loca

© *Mon–Sat, 10am–6pm; Sun, 12pm–5pm*

# Shop

## SECONDHAND

### 13 O'Clock Boutique
**102 Merrion Centre**
**(0113) 243 2776**

This is one of those places where the 50s, 60s and 70s went to die. Selling a range of vintage clothing, from sharp shoes to swinging shirts, a visit to this store is sure to bring out the Austin Powers in even the most Von-Dutched of you. Not only that, but they also do a nice line in retro furniture and accessories, so you'll find everything you need to kit out your pad, should you choose to embark on a full-time career as an international man of mystery. Groovy baby, yeah.

ⓒ *Mon–Thu, 11am–5.30pm; Fri–Sat, 11am–6pm*

### Blue Rinse
**11 Call Lane**
**(0113) 245 1735**

Blue Rinse caters for all your vintage needs, be it old-skool sports wear, period dresses or funky, retro accessories. Unfortunately they've increased their prices considerably since Topshop jumped on the secondhand bandwagon, but it's still an absolute gem. A word of warning though: a piece of clothing being over thirty years old is no guarantee that you'll look good in it; remember that fashions change because things stop looking good. Some of the stock is suitable only for the clinically insane, though we know that's probably an incentive for some of you.

ⓒ *Mon–Fri, 10.30am–6pm; Sat, 10am–6pm; Sun, 11am–4.30pm*

### Sugar Shack
**No. 14 Headingley Lane**
**(0113) 226 1020**

The Sugar Shack is an institution for the students of Leeds. Whether you enter in search of fancy dress, flared cords, a denim mini or even a pair of edible candy undies, the Shack will kit you out and send you off with a hippy skip in your step and the coolest, brightest carrier bag in town. And for those of you who are susceptible to full memory loss after a night on the town, one of their LS6 t-shirts should ensure your taxi driver dumps you somewhere in the vicinity of the slug-infested slum you call home. Just make sure you don't misread it in your drunken state and start licking your clothes.

ⓒ *Mon–Sat, 10am–6pm*

# Shop

## SHOES

### Barratts Factory Outlet
**385 Kirkstall Road, Kirkstall Industrial Park**
**(0113) 239 9880**

You love shoes but have debts like Leeds United. Never mind. BFO will sell you four shiny pairs for a tenner. Fantastic.

*Mon–Sat, 9-30am–5.30pm; Sun, 11am–4pm*

### Office
**74 Briggate**
**(0113) 247 1112**

Still the best place for all your general cool needs. Office do everything from high heels to old-school sneakers, and of course, the odd shoe you can wear to the office.

*Mon–Sat, 9am–6pm; Thu, 9am–7pm; Sun, 11am–5pm*

### Puliga
**176 Harrogate Road, Chapel Allerton**
**(0113) 269 6000**

Puliga sells fabulous Italian and Spanish shoes that guarantee wealth, health and happiness. Okay, maybe not, but they'll make your feet look damn fine.

*Mon–Wed, 10am–5.30pm; Thu–Fri, 10am–6pm; Sat, 10am–5.30pm; Sun, closed*

### Size
**49–51 Vicar Lane**
**(0113) 243 2221**

Size isn't everything, as your poorly endowed ex-boyfriend used to say. Maybe not but they sell some great trainers, and the prices are smaller then he was.

*Mon–Wed, 9.30am–6pm; Thu–Sat, 9.30am–6.30pm; Sun, 11am–5pm*

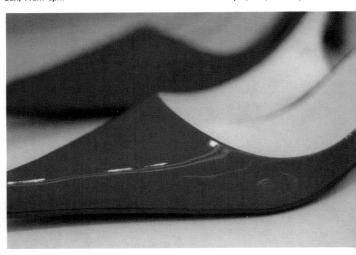

THIS IS A LIMITED EDITION
VINYL. GOT IT FROM A SHOP
IN THE CORN XCHANGE.

# SHOP DIFFERENT.
# LEAVE THE HIGH STREET BEHIND.

**3 CAFE BARS AND 40 INDEPENDENT FASHION, MUSIC AND LIFESTYLE OUTLETS.**

## CORN|XCHANGE

CALL LANE  LEEDS LS1  WWW.CORNX.NET

# Shop

## BOOKS

### Blackwell's
**21 Blenheim Terrace**
**(0113) 243 2446**

Located directly opposite Leeds University, you'll see students outside deliberating whether to plough their money into their studies or reckless beer consumption. Avoid this shop if you're allergic to anyone without a job. Attend if you enjoy the spectator sport of seeing distressed university types trying to buy out-of-stock books because they were too lazy to get their arses down to the library before their entire reading lists were snapped up by more conscientious coursemates.

**☻ Mon & Wed–Sat, 9am–5.30pm;
Tue, 9.30am–5.30pm**

### Oxfam Books
**9 Otley Road, Headingley**
**(0113) 274 3818**

Don't be fooled into thinking that Oxfam shops still sell paintings of crying clowns, Kenny G cassette tapes and the piss-marinated clothes of the recently deceased. They have gone all up-market these days. This branch seems to be where Headingley's students donate their unread textbooks after spending three years drinking themselves into oblivion. As such, it is a great place to buy secondhand books in excellent condition, especially for your course. By buying your reading matter here, you will also be supporting the building of theme parks and Wetherspoons pubs in Africa.

**☻ Mon–Sat, 9.30am–5pm; Sun, 11am–3pm**

### Waterstones
**36–38 Albion Street**
**(0113) 244 0839**

The success of Waterstones is in part thanks to their '3-4-2' offer. Most of the books included in this promotion appear to be novels recommended by smug duo Richard and Judy. Despite being influenced by the most mismatched couple since Bruce Forsythe got together with Miss World, it cannot be refuted that for stock, genre specialisations and customer service, Waterstones sprinkles wee on its rivals from quite a height. The smaller of the two stores has a more efficient book ordering service as well as an impressively stocked cult section.

**☻ Mon–Fri, 8.45am–8pm; Sat,
8.45am–6.30pm; Sun, 11am–5pm**

## MUSIC

### Crash

**35 The Headrow**
**(0113) 243 6743**

The Tardis of Leeds's record shops, Crash packs thousands of digital coasters into its small but beautiful space. Specialising in alternative music, it seems to pander to the purse strings of nu-metal teen goths. Expect to encounter gangs of youngsters in black band t-shirts with piercings and make-up that not even Mary Whitehouse would be shocked by anymore. Crash is the place to go for a friendly atmosphere and cut-price CDs. And contrary to popular myth, it isn't named after the film about people who get turned on by car pile-ups.

🕒 *Mon–Fri, 9.30am–6pm; Sat, 9am–6pm*

### Jumbo

**Unit 5, St Johns Centre, Merrion Street**
**(0113) 245 5570**

Opened in 1971, Jumbo has become something of a legend amongst alternative music fans. Located in the almost completely pointless St Johns Centre, it has a truly local flavour, with staff who know what they are talking about. It manages to avoid the snobby offishness that often accompanies specialist record shops (see Jack Black in *High Fidelity*). With a great stock of imports and promos, Jumbo excels thanks to its eclectic range. Perfect if you need to acquire that Bikini Kill 7-inch or the Kent Northern Soul compilation that has been evading you on eBay recently.

🕒 *Mon–Fri, 9.30am–5.30pm;*
*Sat, 9am–5.30pm*

### Music Zone

**69 The Briggate**
**(0113) 245 4811**

How do they do it? We simply can't think of an explanation for quite how amazing the prices here are. Cheap as chips, it is the sort of place where you can get three top CDs and still have change from a twenty. If a hoity-toity, slightly pretentious atmosphere is more important to you than price, then you should probably nip down to Harvey Nic's where you can get excited about the old fella in a top hat who opens the door for you. But if you just want enough moolah left over at the end of the week to drink yourself into A&E, Music Zone could well be your sort of shop.

🕒 *Mon–Fri, 9am–5.30pm; Sat, 9am–6pm*
*Sun, 11am–5pm*

# Shop

## OTHER

### Anti-Gravity
**Corn Exchange, Call Lane**
**(0113) 245 1735**

If your health-freak of a flatmate is sick of watching her apples bouncing around the kitchen as you attempt to improve your juggling skills, a visit to this place may be in order. Catering for all your clown-related needs, you can buy anything from juggling balls to a unicycle, which might be just the thing for avoiding those rush-hour queues. They'll also give you advice on how to use your new purchases, so if you've failed your degree and are considering running away with the circus, speak to these guys first.

ⓒ *Mon–Sat, 10am–5.30pm; Sun, 11.30am–4.30pm*

### The Condom Shop
**The Corn Exchange, Call Lane**
**(0113) 244 6532**

Playing it safe has never been so much fun. With every colour, size and flavour of condom imaginable you'll be spoilt for choice. They've got the lot here, from rum'n'raisin to glow-in-the-dark, and a few weirder models to keep you giggling as you roll around. It's not all raunchy rubbers though. A whole array of rampant accessories are also on sale here, including drinking games, a variety of vibrators, penis pasta (perfect for when granny pays a visit) and a selection of birthday cards that would even make Jordan blush.

ⓒ *Mon–Sat, 9.30am–5.30pm; Sun, 10.30am–4.30pm*

### Fit to Bust
**6 Stainbeck Corner, Chapel Allerton**
**(0113) 307 0011**

You're going out on a work's do, so you've bought a whole outfit in order to impress that Johnny Depp look-alike from the office. Looking great and feeling fine, you're getting all the right signals, so you go in for the kill. Before you know where you are, you're back at his place. It is at this point, you realise you're wearing some three-year-old granny knickers from M&S. At one point they must have been white but now they're a kind of elephant grey. You panic, burst into tears and run out into the night. Next time, make sure you visit Fit to Bust. Underwear that'll support you in all the right ways.

ⓒ *Mon–Sat, 10am–6pm*

## Hippypottermouse

**Corn Exchange, Call Lane**

**(0113) 467 265**

If Coldplay's Chris Martin were to do his shopping in Leeds, you'd probably find him in this place eyeing up their fair trade clothing. This is the longest established New Age shop in the city and they've got your ethically-sound sartorial needs fully covered, meaning you can leave your conscience at home for the afternoon while you indulge your inner shopaholic. So if you're a bit of a hippy at heart why not pop in. It might also be worth a visit if you're fella's a bit of a flop in the bedroom, as it sells books completely devoted to love potions. Then again, a trip to Ann Summers might be a safer bet.

◉ *Mon–Sat, 9.30am–5.30pm*

## Org Organics

**2 Queen Victoria Street, Victorian Quarter**

**(0113) 234 7000**

You've been caning it so much recently that you've started hallucinating. Either that or Winston Churchill was lurking behind the dustbins when you took the rubbish out earlier. It's time to start taking your health then seriously and where better to start than Org Organics? This totally organic zone will soon have you full of chemical-free vitamins and nutrients. There's even a holistic treatment centre where they will do their best to soothe your broken mind. If you're too scared to venture outside for fear of bumping into Mr Churchill again though, they also provide a home delivery service.

◉ *Mon–Fri, 9.30am–5.30pm; Sat, 10am–5pm*

## K.O.O.L.

**Corn Exchange, Call Lane**

**(0113) 246 9210**

What do ex-*Big Brother* contestants do when they're released back into the wild? Well, they might try a bit of TV presenting, release an exercise video or if we're lucky, they just vanish into complete and utter obscurity. Justine Sellman – BB4, as if you needed reminding – has tried to extend her 15 minutes of fame by branching out into fashion retail. To be fair, she hasn't done too bad a job of it; this high quality boutique in the Corn Exchange stocks a fantastic range of clothes, handbags and jewellery. Perhaps you just get a higher calibre of reality TV star in Leeds.

◉ *Mon–Sat, 10am–5.30pm; Sun, 12pm–4pm*

# Out & About

# Out & About

## CINEMA

### Cottage Road Cinema
**7 Cottage Road**
**(0113) 275 1606**

Succesfully screening flicks since 1912, this place is much more mainstream than the Hyde Park Picture House. But with charming décor, old-fashioned ambiance and a quaint loyalty to the Saturday afternoon matinee, this is a cinema we think is definitely worth supporting. And, contrary to local folklore, it's named after the road it sits on, rather than the fact that George Michael once came here to watch a film.

🎬 *Screenings: Mon–Fri, 6pm & 8.30pm; Sat, 11am & 2pm; Sun, 3pm*

🎟 £3–4.50

### Hyde Park Picture House
**Brudenell Road, Hyde Park**
**(0113) 275 2045**

The Picture House is a famous Leeds landmark, screening independent, art-house, classic and foreign films as well as the occasional blockbuster. The silent films with accompanying live organ music are a particular treat. Built in 1908, the place has a charming dilapidated grandeur with its original gas lighting and a decorated Edwardian balcony. The décor, crusty seats, damp toilet and odd bout of dodgy projection, gives you the feeling that you are in an old porn cinema in 1960's Soho, but without the dirty old men fiddling with their unmentionables inside raincoats.

🎬 *Doors open: Fri, 6pm; Sat, 12pm; Sun, 4pm*

🎟 £4–4.50

## COMEDY

### Hyena Lounge
**The Oak, Headingley**
**(0113) 275 1322**

Wicked little comedy venue run by some very well-connected people who are passionate about quality live comedy. The Hyena Lounge has managed to attract some pretty heavyweight names over the years, as well as launching new fledging acts to the scene by giving up-and-coming acts a chance on stage. Even though they're only open once a week, this is far and away the best laugh in town, apart from the time your best mate found a cockroach's head in his half-eaten kebab

🎬 *Doors open: Thu, 8pm*

🎟 £5

## THEATRE

### City Varieties Music Hall

**Swan Street**

**(0113) 243 0808**

If you're one of those people who bemoans the passing of the golden age of variety performers, this could well be the place for you. The emphasis here is still very much on doing things the old-fashioned way. Be it laughs, dancing, or a decent 'roll aht va barrel...' sing-a-long, you'll get it with bells on here. So by all means come along and enjoy some Butlins-stylee entertainment. But if Bruce Forsythe refuses to die and Shane Ritchie stays on our screens, you've only got yourself to blame.

☻ *Doors open: 7.30pm*

🎟 *£6–15*

### West Yorkshire Playhouse

**Playhouse Square**

**(0113) 213 7700**

If you've made the mistake of watching University Challenge and have been left feeling like the thickest, most uncultured excuse of a human being ever to have been born without being immediately drowned in a bucket, the West Yorkshire Playhouse could well prove to be your salvation. It's one of the best regional theatres in the country and hosts some fantastic productions. A trip here will guarantee you'll have something to talk about to your mates, other than the latest antics of *Emmerdale* scatter Cain Dingle.

☻ *Doors open: 7pm; Matinées and signed performances also available*

🎟 *From £7*

### Leeds Metropolitan University Theatre

**Woodhouse Lane**

**(0113) 283 5998**

Come and watch a bunch of drama students give it their all while they're still young, idealistic and full of hope (before they realise they're destined for a life of flipping burgers in McDonalds). Actually, it's not all as demoralising as that. They put on some pretty decent performances, and as it's slightly cheaper to get a good seat for a show here than at a proper grown-up theatre, it's a great place to come and see a well-produced play and still have enough money for a gin and tonic at half time.

☻ *Doors open: 7.30pm*

🎟 *Adults £7; Conc, £5*

# Out & About

## GALLERIES

### Leeds City Art Gallery

**The Headrow**

**(0113) 247 8248**

Think enjoying art is about mincing around in roll-neck sweaters, stroking your wispy beard? A stroll around the City Gallery will soon convince you that painting and stuff isn't just for the pretentious few. Free entry means you can explore in ten-minute chunks, rather than making your visit feel like an endless school trip. It's particularly strong on British Modernist painting, and sculpture, thanks to its links with the Henry Moore Institute next door.

Ⓒ *Mon–Sat, 10am–5pm; Wed, 10am–8pm; Sun, 1pm–5pm*

Ⓔ *Free*

### Henry Moore Institute

**74 The Headrow**

**(0113) 234 3158**

The clinically elegant black-marble exterior of the Henry Moore Institute doesn't exactly scream 'welcome'. Neither do the bored-brainless gallery assistants whose sole purpose seems to be to smirk at anything you say about art that's not worthy of *The South Bank Show*. Anyway, if you're self-assured enough to deal with this, then the institute is worth a gander. It usually houses touring exhibitions and, like the great man himself, is largely concerned with sculpture. Entry is free and if you want more once you've seen everything, Leeds City Art Gallery is just next door.

Ⓒ *Mon–Sun, 10am–5.30pm; Wed, 10am–9pm*

Ⓔ *Free*

### Yorkshire Sculpture Park

**West Bretton, Wakefield**

**(01924) 832 631**

If you find yourself on the verge of battering a little old lady to death with your box of Findus crispy pancakes because she insists on standing as close as humanly possible to you in the checkout queue at Morrissons, it sounds like you need a break from city life. The Yorkshire Sculpture Park offers 500 acres of good ol' Mother Nature, punctuated with a bit of culture. And if it's raining there's always the Longside Gallery.

Ⓒ *Summer (Apr–Oct), Grounds and Centre, 10am–6pm; Indoor galleries, 11am–5pm; Winter (Nov–Mar), Grounds and Centre, 10am–5pm; Indoor galleries, 11am–4pm*

Ⓔ *Free*

## MUSEUMS

### Royal Armouries

Armouries Drive
(08700) 344 344

Fancy finding out about butt kicking medieval style? The Royal Armouries has five fascinating galleries: War, Tournament, Self Defence, Hunting and Oriental. Essentially a huge collection of the various implements that people have used to kill other people, and the odd animal, from the Dark Ages to the present day. It's all presented in a pretty interesting way, including live accounts and jousting demonstrations, so you might learn something while satisfying your blood lust.

🕐 *Mon–Sun, 10am–5pm*
💷 *Free*

### Thackray Medical Museum

Beckett Street
(0113) 244 4343

This place is a testament to the good ol' days when people simply took a swig of vodka and had both legs amputated with a rusty saw, before returning to work down the pit the same afternoon. Itchy recommends a walk through the giant replica gut they built with a £3 million lottery grant. Also worth a peek is the pain, pus and blood exhibition, though if you're the sort of person who feels faint at the sight of a medium rare steak it may not be advisable to try this one just after lunch. Take a sick bag.

🕐 *Mon–Sun, 10am–6pm*
*(last admission, 5.30pm)*
💷 *£3.50*

### Tropical World

Canal Gardens, Roundhay Park
(0113) 266 1850

Come down and visit a piece of the tropical rainforest right here in Leeds. Home to 40 different varieties of butterfly, some weird and wonderful fish and the only nocturnal species of monkey in the world. They've built it so you walk around under the dripping leaves, while the little critters flutter, splash and rustle about all around you. If you're still suffering the effects of last night's... errr... exotic behaviour, you get to sweat out some toxins too. Better than your average greenhouse.

🕐 *Mon–Sun, 10am–6pm*
*(last admission, 5.30pm)*
💷 *£3*

# Out & About

## LIVE MUSIC

### Brudenell Social Club
33 Queens Road, Hyde Park
(0113) 275 2411

Although this place is more *Phoenix Nights* than Caesar's Palace, it's still an excellent venue for bands. It's the kind of place you can imagine entering through the kitchen, shouting hello to the chef and being seated at the front because you're a personal friend of the owner, like Henry Hill in *Goodfellas*. We wouldn't recommend trying this though, as you'll only get thrown out on your ear by that burly barmaid with the tattoos.

 Mon–Fri, 4pm–11pm; Sat, 12pm–11pm; Sun, 12pm–10.30pm; Gigs from 7.30pm
 £5–£7

### HiFi
2 Central Road
(0113) 242 7353

The HiFi used to be a closely guarded secret amongst the kind of people who are able to reel off every B-side and limited-edition 12-inch released by any band you care to name in the history of the world, as long as they'd never had a top-forty hit. Now, even people who've heard of Robbie Williams manage to sneak in. So, why not leave the white stilettos and glittery boob tube at home and treat yourself to a bit of live jazz, funk, soul or hip hop at what is possibly the best club in Leeds.

 Mon–Wed, 10pm–2am; Thu, 10pm–2.30am; Fri–Sat, 10pm–3am; Sun, 12pm–12.30am
 Prices vary

### The Cockpit
Swinegate
(0113) 244 1573

Contrary to popular myth, the Cockp is not a venue for gay, Roman-sty orgies in the manner of Frankie Goes T Hollywood's *Relax* video. You think we tell you about it if it was? The name actual comes from its previous incarnation a the Cock of the North pub (and no, we' not talking about Chris Moyles). It's a excellent music venue for bands too sma to play either of the universities. Boastin a variety of club nights, the Cockp pumps out a heady mix of rock, met ska, punk, classic indie, new wave ar other things that are difficult to dance t

 Gigs from 7.30pm
 £4–£16

### Joseph's Well
Chorley Lane
(0113) 203 1861

The cheap as chips gigs at this plac means you can afford to go and see band you've never heard of. This can b a bit like pearl diving, or in some case Russian roulette. However, it's wor taking the risk because amongst all th teenagers aping whoever is on the fro of the *NME*, you might just come acros a talented local band that is really goir places. You can then chat up the lea guitarist, get married within the mon and, when the band are offered a mul million-pound recording deal, quit yo job and set up home on easy stre

 Gigs from 7pm
 £3–£7

## Leeds Metropolitan University Student Union

**Calverley Street**

**(0113) 283 2600**

The Met's union bar (or LMUSU, to give it its rather snappy acronym) is in many ways the kooky, cutting edge little sister of the other University's union (the LUU – keep up). It's a slightly smaller venue attracting slightly smaller names at vastly cheaper prices. The students in this place might all be doing courses in sport and meedja but they have a much cooler spot to see bands than their poncier counterparts up the road, and besides, who goes to university to learn anything anyway?

*Opening times vary*

*From £6*

## The Wardrobe

**St Peter's Building, St Peter's Square**

**(0113) 383 8800**

Although the underground club here looks like the perfect setting for a bare-knuckle fist-fighting competition, don't let that put you off. There are few greater pleasures to be had in this fair city than a night of live music at the Wardrobe. Whether you're shaking to funk, finger-clicking to jazz or shoe-shuffling to soul, the acts are always top quality and a fun night is sure to be had by all. Check with the venue for listings, as they put a stack of diverse stuff on and we wouldn't want you to miss a trick.

*Fri–Sat, 10pm–2.30am*

*Prices vary*

## The Packhorse

**208 Woodhouse Lane**

**(0113) 245 3980**

If you've ever done the Otley run, you'll probably have been in this place but as it's one of the last pubs in the run, chances are your memories of it will be pretty hazy, and as you were probably regurgitating your 28th pint at the time it's unlikely you'll have noticed the gig venue upstairs – it's definitely worth knowing about though. Despite the fact that it's usually filled with student bands and their mates, you'll still get to hear some quality sounds. Just be prepared to have snakebite and black spilt down your back while you get as sweaty as Rick Waller's jockstrap.

🎵 *Gigs from 7pm*

💷 *£2–5*

# Out & About

## SPORT

### AMF Bowling

**Merrion Centre, Merrion Way**
**(0845) 658 1271**

Put on some silly shoes and throw huge, coloured, plastic balls at faraway skittles.

☉ *Sun–Fri, 9.30am–12am; Sat, 9.30am–12.30am*
🅱 *From £2.80; Shoe hire, £1*

### Hollywood Bowl

**Cardigan Fields Road, Kirkstall Road**
**(0113) 279 9111**

Think you're a bigger bowling talent than Lebowski? Then you need to head here dude, and do your thing on the lanes. Just don't overdo the Caucasians.

☉ *Mon–Sun, 10am–12am*
🅱 *From £2.60*

### Headingley Cricket Ground

**St Michael's Lane**
**(0113) 278 7394**

Full of old Yorkies moaning about 'Poor boolin', and roaring 'Yooooaaaaarkshare'. They'll also be reminiscing about sheep they've loved and lost and five pound notes they've had all their lives.

🅱 *From £12*

### Leeds Rhinos

**St Michael's Lane**
**(0845) 278 6181**

The Rhinos continue their domination of Super League at the mo, stampeding all opposition in their path. So why not soak up the carnival atmosphere, while grown men get muddy for your pleasure.

🅱 *From £12*

# FOOTBALL

**UP NORTH, THERE'S LIFE AND DEATH, AND THEN THERE'S FOOTBALL.**

Leeds United has a chequered history, and when you look at recent controversy you have only to remember that even its founding was a shady affair. Its predecessor, Leeds City, was caught making dodgy payments to ringers back in 1919 and the resulting fines and expulsion from the league sounded its death knell. Off the back of this, the new club, Leeds United, was founded, and it's lived on the edge ever since. Crippling debts and relegation from the premiership a couple of years back left the club teetering on extinction, and all this on the back of a Champions League semi-final. Throughout it all, the faithful fans have stuck by the 'Mighty Whites' with an almost unquestioning faith. Aaaaah.

Paul Bracewell is in charge of team affairs, with the irrepressible chairman Ken Bates taking over in the board room, dispensing with the goldfish tanks and providing stability.

Marching on together, the glory days will come again.

**Leeds United FC**
Elland Road
(0845) 121 1992
Tickets £20-45

# Out & About

## FURTHER AFIELD

### Fountains Abbey & Studley Royal Water Garden
**Ripon**
**(01765) 608 888**

In 1132, 13 monks decided there must be more to life than playing bullshit bingo during their abbot's soul-destroyingly long sermons and left to set up on their own. They left behind the most complete Cistercian abbey remains in Britain today. Among the delights on offer here is a wild deer park, providing ample opportunity for you to scare your partner with the classic, 'When are we going to have a baby, dear?'

⊙ *Fountains Abbey, Hall and Water Garden, Nov–Feb, 10am–4pm; Mar–Oct, 10am–5pm;*
⊞ *£5.50*

### Lightwater Valley
**North Stainley, Ripon**
**(0870) 458 0040**

Conquering the Falls of Terror, being forced to endure Trauma Tower and then coming face to face with the Grizzly Bear might not sound like a fun day out, but you'd be wrong. These are just three of the jaw-dropping/pant-wrecking rides at the adrenaline junkie's paradise Lightwater Valley. With Europe's longest rollercoaster The Ultimate, and the biggest swing boat in Britain, The Wave, it might not be a great day out if you're still wrestling with the mother of all hangovers. After all, no one enjoys being reacquainted with last night's chicken rogan josh.

⊙ *Rides and attractions, 10.30am–4.30pm*
⊞ *£13.95–15.50*

### Scarborough

Scarborough: sun, sea and sex. Only without the sex or the sun. But don't let that put you off. Donkeys, amusement arcades, ice cream, miniature golf, pterodactyl-sized seagulls, open-top buses and lashings of fish and chips all contribute to a good old-fashioned seaside resort. In a world full of high tech gadgetry, the Naval Battle at Peasholm Park will delight technophobes with its complete lack of innovation in the last 50 years, and the more adventurous can always dip a big toe in the North Sea if they feel nature calling. Scarborough is still special because it sticks to a simple principle that's been around longer than people have been spending Sunday afternoons here: if it aint broke.

## TOURIST ATTRACTIONS

### Kirkstall Abbey
Abbey Road (A65), 3 miles west of Leeds city centre
(0113) 230 5492

One Thursday evening a long time ago, a group of friars were bored (the storyline in *Eastenders* was dull that week) so they decided to build a monastery. Sadly, once it was built, *Eastenders* started to get a bit more interesting and the whole thing fell into disrepair. These days the abbey is undergoing long-term restoration and is closed to the public. Nevertheless the grounds are still pretty impressive and this is a great place to laze on a sunny afternoon.

*Museum, Tue–Sat, 10am–5pm; Sun, 1pm–5pm; Abbey, dawn to dusk*

*Free*

### Meanwood Valley Urban Farm
Sugar Well Road, Meanwood
(0113) 262 9759

Farmers are a lazy bunch, aren't they? The government pay them millions of pounds a year to play around on their combine harvesters all day long, and all they're expected to do in return is to feed a few boxy animals. But some of them, it would seem, can't even be bothered to do that and instead they charge gullible city folk to do it for them. Let Old MacDonald do his own work, we say. And while you're at it, you can get off our land. Bloody country folk, coming here with fancy country ways, telling us how to live our lives...

*Mon–Sun, 9am–4pm*

*£1*

### Roundhay Park
**Princess Avenue**
(0113) 266 1850

The perfect venue for a romantic stroll with the focus of your affections. Gaze longingly at her as you amble by the lake, or whisper sweet nothings in his ear while you walk arm-in-arm past the ornamental blooms of Canal Gardens. And if 700 acres of fields, flowers, trees and other bits and pieces of nature don't get your beau in the mood for a quick fumble in the bushes, you can always take him/her/it to the Roundhay Fox. We've found that a few glasses of their excellent vino usually work wonders before getting down to a proper romp in the country.

*Free*

# Out & About

## OTHER

### Café Thai Cookery Lessons

**Chinatown Shopping Arcade**
**(0800) 083 5552**

If you've always yearned to know the difference between a green curry and a red one (and which one will massacre your mates' taste buds) then Café Thai host lessons in Thai cookery. You can either do one-offs or sign up to their full six-week course. With any luck, at some point they'll teach you how to make a massaman like you had that time on Koh Tao. Or if you really can't get the hang of it, you could always head down to the restaurant afterwards to taste it how it should be done by people who know how to cook without burning things.

*Call for info*

### Xscape

**Colorado Way, Glasshoughton**
**(01765) 200 322**

It's not just posh people who can enjoy skiing, you know. Oh no. The high life is open to everyone, even us northerners. In fact, it's right on our doorstep. Well, Castleford anyway. And Xscape has it all: a real snow slope, an ice wall, a rock climbing wall, an aerial assault course, an all-weather skatepark, dodgems, a 20 lane bowling alley and a laser adventure zone. And when you're suffering after last night's binge fest, there's even a 14 screen cinema where you are free to collapse in the dark and concentrate on whether or not eating a piece of popcorn will make you throw up what remains of your liver.

*Mon–Sat, 9am–11.30pm; Sun, 10am–11pm*

# STAG AND HEN NIGHTS

BREAK OUT THE L-PLATES AND LOCK UP YOUR DAUGHTERS. HERE'S ITCHY'S GUIDE TO YOUR FINAL NIGHT OF FREEDOM...

Cooooo-eeeeee big boy!

## Go Ballistic Paintball

Newton Street
Bradford
(0870) 141 7490

So your best mate's marrying your ex. Take a deep breath, book a day's entertainment at this indoor stadium and shoot the shit out of him in one of their famous 'stag hunts.'

## The Condom Shop

The Corn Exchange
(0113) 244 6532

Three guesses what these people sell. Organic cereals? Children's books? Or stacks of prophylactics, mysterious devices and filth-related novelties? Why not use them in place of confetti on the big day?

Bucking brilliant!

## Walkabout

Cookridge Street
(0113) 205 6500

Or Crawlabout by the time you emerge from the dunnies in the wee small hours. Cheap alcopops and a nice big dance floor where Chesney will remind you that you are the one and only.

## The Birdcage

52 Boar Lane
(0113) 246 7273

Probably more one for the hens than the stags this, but with an open mind (and we're talking 24-hour Tesco) there isn't a night out in Leeds to match it. Miss Orry and her gang of dancing vixens will woo you with happy-hour drinks and weekend drag and cabaret shows. As you might imagine they're well versed in pre-nup giggles and if you book in advance, they'll provide a free bottle of bubbly for each group of six. Drink, dance and do whatever you like, just don't touch Miss Orry's hair – each wig costs around four grand.

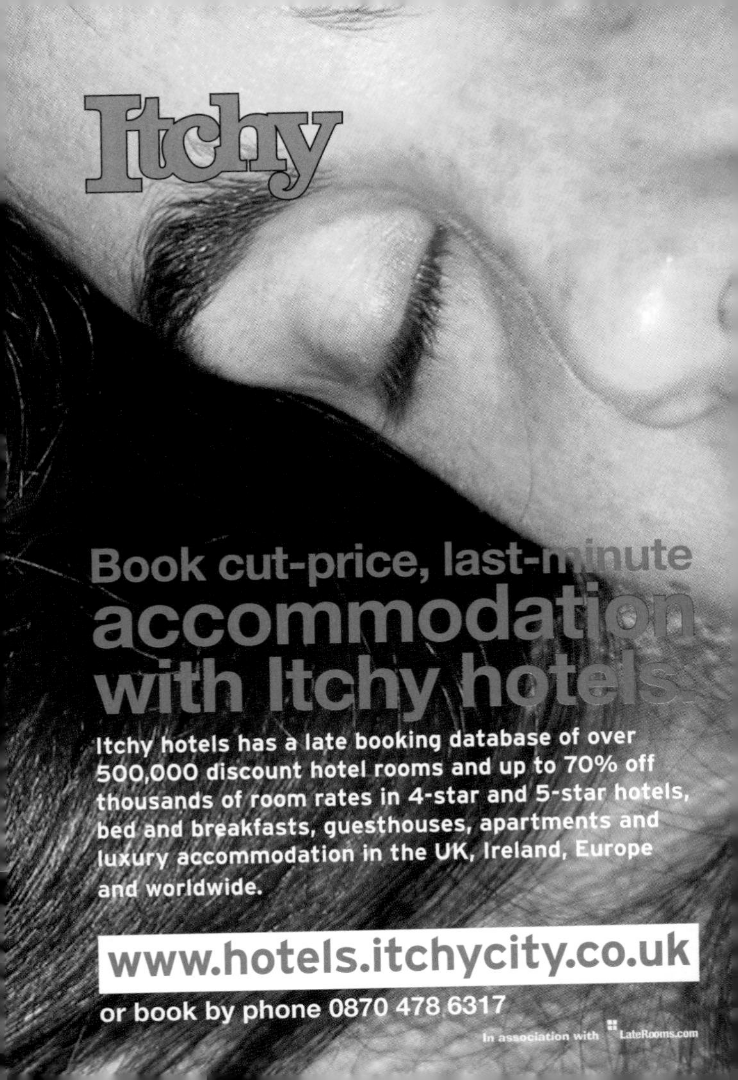
Itchy
Book cut-price, last-minute
accommodation
with Itchy hotels
Itchy hotels has a late booking database of over 500,000 discount hotel rooms and up to 70% off thousands of room rates in 4-star and 5-star hotels, bed and breakfasts, guesthouses, apartments and luxury accommodation in the UK, Ireland, Europe and worldwide.
www.hotels.itchycity.co.uk
or book by phone 0870 478 6317
In association with LateRooms.com

# Laters

# Laters

## Post-work beauty boost

You catch a glimpse of your reflection in a shop window after leaving work and realise you look like a washed out Marilyn Manson. You need help before you start scaring small children in the street. Treat yourself to a beauty fix at Hanalee in The Light (0113 244 9898). Open 'til 8pm on Thursdays and 7pm on Fridays.

## Late-night shopping

The Leeds 'Alive After Five' initiative means many city centre retailers are keeping their doors open to shoppers 'til 7pm on Thursday, Friday and Saturday evenings. Which means you have the opportunity to hammer those credit cards for an extra few hours a day. Go on, live the consumer dream.

## Café culture

If you're the sort of person who's body clock is 12 hours out of synch with the rest of the world, you're going to need your early morning coffee a little later than most people. Luckily for you, L'Organise Café on Hyde Park Corner keeps serving cappuccinos and lattés way after 11pm on Friday and Saturday nights.

## After-hours culture

If you're feeling brain dead after your boss has had you counting paper clips at work all day, take yourself along to the City Gallery for a bit of stimulation. Open 'til 8pm on a Wednesday. And if after that you're still in the mood for art, the Henry Moore Institute next door stays open 'til 9pm.

## Drinking 'til the early hours

Ok, so it's a Monday night and you probably shouldn't stay out drinking til two but you're bloody well going to anyway. As any self-respecting liver-hater will tell you, the only place to head is Call Lane. The Elbow Rooms (0113 245 7011), Revolution (0113 243 2778) and Norman (0113 234 3988) all stay open 'til the early hours every night from Monday through to Saturday. If you're already too drunk to walk, or you just can't be bothered to leave the comfort of your own home, the nice people at GimmeSomeBeer (0845 6444 388) will deliver booze, chocolate and ciggies to your door round the clock. All of which means you really have no excuse to be sensible and take it easy.

## Activities for night owls

Insomniacs, don't lie awake tossing and turning all night, get yourself down to Riley's Pool and Snooker Club. They're open 24-hours-a-day, so you can go and hone your cue-handling skills any time of day or night. With all that extra practice, you could well become the next Ronnie O'Sullivan. Then, when you've made your millions, you can fritter it all away at Gala (0113 389 3700) or Grosvenor (0113 269 5051) casino until 6am from Sunday to Friday. If you don't agree with gambling for moral reasons, there's no need for you to cut your night short though. Head down to Blue Leopard (0113 245 5103) where you can watch girls engage in the much more wholesome act of stripping for money until 2.30am during the week, or 4am at weekends.

### Finding fags at 4am

As usual you've left your latest assignment for work until the last minute. You're going to be up all night and you're going to need fags. Lots of fags. Tong Road Total Garage is open all night as is the garage on Cardigan Road, so there's absolutely no reason why you shouldn't have lung cancer by the time the sun comes up.

### Clubbing 'til dawn

If you're only just getting warmed up by 2am and your dancing shoes need a few more hours out of their box, Glass House at Mission (0870 122 0114) runs from 2.30am–9am once a month on Saturday night. Failing that, we've heard rumours that Adel Woods plays host to the odd illegal rave, but of course, that's all we know.

### Food to your door

If you've fallen asleep in the bath and it's too late to cook your own tea, you'l be glad to hear that The Fortune Cookie (08000 155 444) delivers quality Chinese chow until 2am. For those who care less about what they put in their mouth Lucky's (0500 113 345) in Hyde Park exists to bring you pizzas and kebabs until 3am.

### After-hours food

Looking for somewhere to get a huge plate of hot, greasy food after a hard night of clubbing? Naffee's (0113 245 3128) in Hyde Park and Tariq's (0113 275 1881) in Headingley keep serving Indian food 'til 3am at the weekend Just the ticket when you've got a bellyful of beer that needs soaking up

# THE MORNING AFTER
## THE NIGHT BEFORE

LATE NIGHT DRINKING'S ALL WELL AND GOOD, BUT WAKING UP THE MORNING AFTER RARELY IS. WITH A BIT OF FORETHOUGHT YOU CAN AVOID A LOT OF PAIN. SO, AS YOU'RE STAGGERING HOME AND THE LIGHT OF THAT LATE-NIGHT SHOP SWIMS INTO FOCUS, GET IN THERE AND GRAB SOME OF THE FOLLOWING ITEMS TO MAKE YOURSELF FEEL BETTER:

**Fruit juice** – Fruity juices contain a good measure of fructose which, helps to burn up alcohol. And it counts as a portion of fruit and veg, so you can repair some of the previous night's damage. Less healthily, you could also pick up one of any number of sugary treats such as Mars bars or sweets. The sugar in them should have the same effect.

**Beans** – Along with rice, grains, cereals, peas and nuts, beans have high levels of Vitamin B1, which helps you to metabolise the booze. It also stabilises the nervous system, as it's a lack of B1 which often causes the shakes.

**Bananas** – Bananas are high in potassium, which your body loses a lot of when you're drinking. Plus they contain high levels of headache-reducing magnesium, and are also a natural antacid which'll help with the nausea.

**Sports cordial** – All the toilet trips you'll have made whilst drunk'll have robbed your body of all its salts, so you'll need the salts contained in sports drinks to redress the balance.

**Eggs** – Eggs contain cysteine which is used by the body to mop up chemicals called free radicals. A decent fry-up often sets you straight in no time at all.

**Tomatoes** – Full of antioxidants and vitamins, you should feel better about 15 minutes after eating them. Tomato juice works just as well. Alternatively, add vodka for a 'hair of the dog' style Bloody Mary.

# Sleep

# Sleep

## EXPENSIVE

### 42 The Calls
42 The Calls
(0113) 244 0099
Luckily for you they're better at giving customers a good night's sleep than coming up with names for hotels.
🅔 *Double rooms, £69*; *Double deluxe, £170*

### Park Plaza
City Square, Boar Lane
(0113) 380 4000
Stylish hotel with fabulous bar and East fusion restaurant. Its location just near the railway station makes it a perfect stopover for new arrivals to Leeds
🅔 *Double rooms, £85–125;*
*Breakfast included*

## MID-RANGE

### Bewley's Hotel
City Walk, Sweet Street
(0113) 234 2340
Bargain prices for a really classy hotel. Internet nuts will be pleased to hear that free broadband access is provided.
🅔 *Double rooms, £69*

### Holiday Inn Express
Cavendish Street
(0113) 242 6200
You can't miss this seven storey leviathan, with it's illuminated blue staircase up one side. Breakfast is free, which is good, because you'll need to get your strength back after going up those stairs.
🅔 *Double rooms from £59*

### Golden Lion
2 Briggate
(0113) 243 6454
Situated near trendy Call Lane, where you can have a rip-roaring good time before heading back to your den. If you want to get your paws on some food, you can do so at the excellent Wharf restaurant
🅔 *Single rooms, £90; Twin rooms, £99*

### Travel Inn
Wellington Street
(0113) 242 8105
Situated next to TGI Fridays, which is handy for guests who like to eat bog-standard food in the company of drunk office workers. Those with more taste can use the free wi-fi to plan a slightly better evening
🅔 *Rooms from £53.95*

## CHEAP

### Butlers Hotel

40 Cardigan Road

(0113) 274 4755

You don't need an aristocratic master to spend a night here, but if you do bring one, leave him at the cricket ground overnight.

**Rooms from £40**

### Clock Hotel

317 Roundhay Road

(0113) 249 0304

You have to hand it to them, these guys know how to treat you right. The beds are the opposite of minute, in fact, hours was huge. There's no doubt they'll be seeing our faces a seconds time.

**Rooms from £45**

### Trafford + Budapest Hotels

12–14 Cardigan Road

(0113) 274 2422

Legend has it that a traveller from Manchester once came here on his way to Hungary, and liked it so much he decided to stay forever. That may not be strictly true, but we're sure you get the idea.

**Rooms from £29; Breakfast included**

### St Michael's Tower Hotel

5 St Michael's Villas, Cardigan Road

(0113) 275 5557

Cardigan Road seems to be a spawning ground for nice little hotels, before they grow up into nasty, sterile places, and go and live near motorways. Let's hope St Michael's Tower Hotel stays young forever.

**Rooms from £48; Breakfast included**

## LETTING AGENTS

### Avtar
127 Brudenell Road
(0113) 274 5111

### King Sturge
Capitol House
(0113) 244 1441

### Park Lane
25–27 Otley Road
(0113) 230 4949
www.parklaneproperties.com

### Redbrick
48 Otley Road
(0113) 230 5552
www.redbrickproperties.com

# Useful info

# Useful info

## BEAUTY SALONS

### Hanalee
Garden Unit, The Light, The Headrow
(0113) 244 9898

'I want to be beautiful,' we hear you say. 'Go to Hanalee,' is all we can say.

Ⓒ *Mon–Wed & Sat, 9am–6pm; Thu, 9am–late; Fri, 9am–7pm; Sun, 11am–5pm*

### Nailcraft
22 The Headrow
(0113) 245 0888

Just found out that your boyfriend has cheated on you again? Cheer yourself up with some brand new nails. Not only do they look good, they're also extremely useful for scratching eyes out with.

Ⓒ *Ring for appointments*

## HEALTH CLUBS

### LA Fitness
6–24 Albion Street
(0113) 163 2047

Is it worth it? Let me work it. You put your thang down, flip it and reverse it.

Ⓒ *Mon–Thu, 6.30am–10pm; Fri, 6.30am–8pm; Sat–Sun, 9am–5pm*

## TATTOO

### Ultimate Skin Tattoo
29a New Briggate
(0113) 244 4940

Meet someone nice in the pub last night? You can get their phone number tattooed on your forehead here. Nice.

Ⓒ *Mon–Sun, 12pm–8pm*

## HAIRDRESSERS

### The Barber Shop
85 Kirkgate
(0113) 246 7587

The place to go for afro, European and mixed hair textures, and hair tattoos.

Ⓒ *Mon–Thu & Sat, 8.30am–5pm; Fri, 8.30am–6pm*

### Box Creative Hairdressing
3 Lower Briggate
(0113) 245 6869

Having a face like a barn can be a disadvantage in life. The trick is to draw people's eyes with your hair. Box Creative specialise in bold colours and cuts

Ⓒ *Mon–Wed & Fri–Sat, 10am–6pm; Thu, 10am–7pm*

## The Hair Studio

4a Otley Road

(0113) 274 0513

Past finalists in the British Hair Awards, your mop's in safe hands here. And if that's not enough, they also give free shiatsu head massages and student discounts.

🕒 Mon–Wed, 9am–6pm; Thu & Fri, 9am–7pm; Sat, 9am–5pm

## The Cutting Room

Town Street, Chapel Allerton

(0113) 269 7070

Go easy when they offer you a free glass of wine in here. If you wake up the next morning with a rainbow mohican, you'll have no one to blame but yourself.

🕒 Mon–Tue, 9am–5pm; Wed, 9am–5.30pm; Thu–Fri, 9am–8pm; Sat, 8.30am–4.30pm

## Expo Hair Design

Unit 2, White Cloth Hall, Crown Street

(0113) 234 7235

Student discounts, plus a student training evening from 4pm every Monday.

🕒 Mon–Wed, 9am–6pm; Thu, 9am–7pm; Fri, 9am–6pm; Sat 9pm–5pm

💷 Men's cuts from £30 and women's cuts from £33 onwards

## Toni & Guy

Bar Lane

(0113) 234 4334

Reputable chain of hair wizards. Just about the only thing they can't do with your hair is make it grow quicker than does already. Swanky stuff indeed.

🕒 Mon–Tue, 9am–5.15pm; Wed–Thu, 9am–45pm; Fri, 9am–6pm; Sat, 9am–5.15pm

Unit 2
White Cloth Hall
Crown Street
Leeds LS2 7DA
0113 234 7235

hair design

# Useful info

## TAXIS

**Amber**
(0113) 263 6445

**Arrow**
(0113) 258 2573

**City Cabs**
(0113) 246 9999

**Premier**
(0113) 288 8333

**Streamline**
(0113) 244 3322

**Telecabs**
(0113) 263 7777

## BUSES

**Black Prince
(Local)**
(0113) 252 6033

**First Leeds
(Local)**
(0113) 381 5550

**Metroline
(Local)**
(0113) 245 7676

**National Express Bookings**
(0870) 580 8080

**Yorkshire Coastliner**
(0113) 244 8976

## TRAINS

### GNER Bookings
(0845) 722 5225

### Metroline
(0113) 245 7676

### Midland Mainline
(0845) 712 5678

### National Rail Enquiries
(0845) 748 4950

### Northern Trains
(0870) 602 3322

### Virgin Trains
(0870) 789 1234

## PLANES

### Leeds Bradford Airport
(0113) 250 9696

Nearer to Leeds, but we don't mind sharing.

### Manchester Airport
(0161) 489 3000

Avoid the locals if you must fly from here.

## USEFUL INFORMATION

### Tourist Information
Leeds City Station

(0113) 242 5242

The first port of call if you have any questions about travel, accommodation, attractions or absolutely anything else your little tourist heart might be yearning for.

# Useful info

## LETTING AGENTS

### City Red Properties
35 Cromer Terrace
(0113) 247 1101

### Leeds Properties
26 Blenheim Terrace
(0113) 237 0000

### Park Lane
172–174 Harrogate Road, Chapel Allerton
(0113) 237 0000
www.parklaneproperties.com
🕒 Mon–Fri, 9am–5.30pm; Sat, 10am–5pm

### Samara
207 Clarendon Road
(0113) 244 2443

## FISH & CHIPS

### Brett's Fish and Chips
14 North Lane, Headingley
(0113) 232 3344
Watch England stuff the Aussies then stuff your face with the finest fish and chips in the whole of Leeds
🕒 Mon–Sun, 11.30am–10pm

### Bryan's of Headingley
9 Weetwood Lane, Headingley
(0113) 278 5679
Apparently, the world's supply of cod and haddock is rapidly dwindling away, so hurry up and get your arse down to Bryan's before they have to resort to selling battered tadpoles
🕒 Mon–Sun, 12pm–10pm

## INDIAN

### Nazam's
201 Woodhouse Street
(0113) 243 8515
You like to eat curry in bed, but Anatole your chef, is on holiday. Easy. As Duggins, your butler, to call Nazam's
🕒 Mon–Fri, 5pm–1am; Sat–Sun, 5pm–2.30am

### New Sultan's
39 New Briggate
(0113) 243 8500
Treat your harem to a delicious dollop of Indian food, without having to leave the comfort of your own palace. After all, if it's good enough for the Sultan it's good enough for the likes of you
🕒 Mon–Fri, 5pm–1am; Sat–Sun, 5pm–2.30am

# Useful info

## ORIENTAL

### Fortune Cookie
**81 Raglan Road, Hyde Park**
**(0800) 155 444**
Wise man, he say when geese fly south you need food in your mouth, river child. He was so right. Delivers.
*Mon–Sat, 5pm–3am; Sun, 5pm–1am*

### Maxi's Express
**23 The Light, The Headrow**
**(0113) 245 7788**
If you've woken up with the mother of all zits on your face and can't bear the thought of leaving the house, you can still enjoy Maxi's quality grub in your own home. Just get a mate to pick it up.
*Mon–Sun, 12pm–10.30pm*

## PIZZA

### Caesar's
**209 Stanningley Road**
**(0113) 279 8888**
Pay tribute to the man who conquered Gaul, sacked Germania, thwarted Hannibal and invented salad. Apparently.
*Mon–Sun, 5pm–12.30am*

### Domino's Pizza
**12 St Anne's Road, Headingley**
**(0113) 289 9559**
If only 'doh' will do, get on the blower to Domino's, and they'll deliver one of their finest creations direct to your home(r). Mmmmm pizza..
*Mon–Thu, 4pm–11pm;*
*Fri–Sat, 12pm–11pm*

### Harpo's
**23 Otley Road, Headingley**
**(0113) 278 2145**
You've left home and you're a bit worried. How will you survive without your mum's cooking? The answer lies at Harpo's where they'll have you feeling at home quicker than you can say Mama Mia.
*Mon–Sun, 5pm–12am*

### Italian Affair
**304 Stanningley Road, Bramley**
**(0113) 256 9955**
You walk in, and a gorgeous waiter winks at you. He brings you a menu and then slips his phone number into your hand. You look back at him and whisper, 'One large pepperoni, please.'
*Sun–Thu, 5pm–10.30pm; Fri–Sat, 5pm–11pm*

# SAFETY

**Police**
Millgarth Police Station, Millgarth Street
(0845) 606 0606

**Accident and emergency**
Leeds General Infirmary, Great George Street
(0113) 243 2799

**Doctor**
Healthcare Ltd, Duncan House
(0113) 244 8866

**NHS dentist**
Park Row Dental Practice, 18 Park Row
(0113) 243 0371

**Family planning**
Sunnybank Clinic, Leeds General Infirmary
(0113) 392 2344

**Rape helpline**
(0113) 224 0058

**Samaritans**
(0845) 790 9090
Emotional support, guidance and counselling, 24-hours-a-day.

**Fire and rescue service**
Leeds Fire Station, Kirkstall Road
(0113) 244 0855

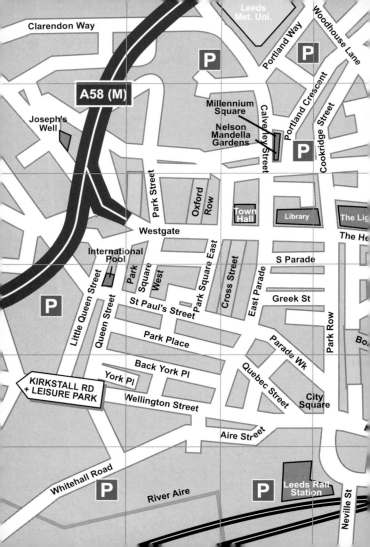

Leeds City Centre

# Index

# Index